Magic Search Words

SCHOLARSHIPS

The Magic Search Word Series

Scholarships
Jobs
Health
Homework
Business
Law
Personal Finance
Animal and Pet Care
Environment

Magic Search Words

SCHOLARSHIPS

Strategies and Search Tactics to Discover the Best of the Internet

Paul J. Krupin

Direct Contact Publishing
Kennewick, Washington

Books are available in quantity for promotional or premium use.
Write to the Director of Special Sales,
Direct Contact Publishing,
P. O. Box 6726, Kennewick, WA 99336,
Email info@MagicSearchWords.com
or call (509) 545-2707.

www.MagicSearchWords.com

ISBN 1–885035–09–8 (softcover)
ISBN 1–885035–13–6 (e-book)

Cover and Interior Design & Typesetting by Desktop Miracles, Inc., Stowe, VT

Library of Congress Cataloging-in-Publication Data

Krupin, Paul J.
    Magic search words: scholarships—strategies and tactics to discover the best of the Internet / Paul J. Krupin
    p. cm.
    ISBN 1–885035–09–8 (softcover)
    ISBN 1–885035–13–6 (e-book)
    1. Scholarships—Computer network resources. 2. Scholarships (Financial Aid)—Computer networks. 3. Internet (Computer network). I. Title. II. Series.
025.06'37 – dc21
LB2338K36 2002

Printed in the United States of America

07 06 05 04 03 02   10 9 8 7 6 5 4 3 2 1

TO ALL THE CHILDREN,
For they shall inherit our knowledge,
hopes, dreams and visions.

Disclaimer

Even a book like this has limitations. This book was written to provide information on the subject of searching and finding information on the Internet. It is sold with the understanding that the publisher and author are not engaged in rendering legal, accounting or other professional services. If expert assistance is required, then the services of a competent professional should be sought.

It is not the intent of this book to cover all the information that is available on this topic from other experts and creative people who also write on this subject. Rather it is intended to complement, amplify, and supplement other available works.

Seeking scholarships is not a guaranteed endeavor. Those who decide this book is for them must expect to invest a lot of time and effort without any guarantee of success. Scholarship applications do not write themselves. Scholarships are not awarded to everyone. To receive a scholarship, one must be among those who applied.

Every effort has been made to make this book complete and as accurate as possible. However, there may be mistakes both typographical and in content. Therefore, this book should only be used as a general guide and not as the ultimate source for information on applying for scholarships. Furthermore, this book only contains information that is current as of the date of printing.

The purpose of this manual is to educate and entertain. The author and publisher shall have neither liability nor responsibility to any person or entity with respect to any loss or damage caused or alleged to be caused directly or indirectly by the information contained in this book.

If you do not wish to be bound by the above, you may return this book to the publisher for a full refund.

If you love to find mistakes, please send in your corrections for the next edition.

Magic Ingredients

Foreword   ix
Preface   xi
Acknowledgments   xiii

CHAPTER 1:   **INTRODUCTION**   1
   • Overview
   • Purpose
   • Getting Started
   • How to Use This Book

CHAPTER 2:   **ALL ABOUT SEARCH ENGINES**   7
   • True Search Engines
   • Web Directories
   • Virtual Libraries
   • Meta-Search Engines
   • The Invisible Web
   • Search Engine Resources

CHAPTER 3:   **THE MAGIC SEARCH WORDS**   15
   • The Search String Technique
      • Simple Searches
      • Advanced Searches
      • Concept and Phrase Searching
   • The Minus Dot Com Trick
   • Magic Search "Learning Words"
   • Magic Search "Internet Words"
   • Special Tactics for Creating Search Strings

CHAPTER 4:   **THE MAGIC SEARCH WORDS KINGDOM**   39
   • Overview of the Kingdom
   • Magic Potions: The Key Search Word String
      Word Groups
   • Magic Spells: Selecting the Magic Search Words

CHAPTER 5:   MAKE A WISH AND CAST A SPELL   49
- Decide What You Want
- Identify Who You Are
- Identify What You Are Interested in
- Identify the Potential Source of Financial Aid
  You Are Interested in
- Identify Where You Want to Be and When
- Research the Media to Identify Potential
  Sources of Information and Contacts

CHAPTER 6:   GETTING SCHOLARSHIPS   77
- Going from Ideas to Action
- The Classical Use of Conventional CBI
- The New Way to Get CBI

CHAPTER 7:   THE MAGIC INCANTATION   83
- The Four Steps: Search, Find, Match & Apply
- Implementing Your Action Plan
- Polish Your Application
- Follow Up
- Use the 3 I Technique

CHAPTER 8:   CONCLUSION   99
- Avoiding Disaster
- Parting Words

APPENDIX A: YOUR SCHOLARSHIP SEARCH ACTION PLAN   103

APPENDIX B: SUMMARY OF THE BEST SCHOLARSHIP
             MAGIC SEARCH WORDS   105

Index   107
Who is Paul J. Krupin?   111

Foreword

by Meryl K. Evans

The Internet and especially its search engines have helped me tremendously in my career as a writer. Without search engines, I would have to spend hours manually tracking down needed information for interviews, articles, reviews, and other writing projects.

Whenever I needed to do research for school, I had to do it the old-fashioned way since it was pre-Internet times. That meant going to the library, organizations, and bookstores to comb for information.

That was barely a decade ago. Phenomenal changes have taken place in the world since I was a student trying to collect the right information to get a good grade. When I entered college, computers weren't quite on every desk. Four years later when I entered the work force, fellow co-workers and I had our own computers.

Just because the search engines and other Internet resources are there for the taking, information won't come to you without your help. Libraries and references still require the crucial and critical skills of knowing how to ask the right questions to search and find the answers.

With search engines having indexed billions of Web pages, it's become a game of looking for a needle in the haystack. We have to give it a hand so it can return the favor of finding what we need without providing irrelevant and overwhelming results.

Online searching is becoming a necessary skill that is in demand for people in all walks of life. It's for the student who is trying to get a good grade on a thesis. It's for the parent who is trying to handle a parenting issue. It's for the professional who is trying to advance in a career. It's for the traveler who is looking for that next exciting destination.

The *Magic Search Words* series provides you with the basic building blocks that expert searchers use. Not only will it give you strategies to support you in your current search efforts, but also it will empower you to learn more and benefit from search engines to help you in other areas of your life.

The book is an incredibly fast read and it'll show you how to conduct effective searches. With a little practice and advice, online searching will become a habit and open new worlds for you.

MERYL K. EVANS
AUTHOR
WWW.MERYL.NET
PLANO, TEXAS

Preface

This book is all about Internet wizardry.

This is not just about technology, but rather the focus is on *YOU*, the person who sits at the computer.

This book teaches *YOU* how to select the right string of words for your search. The words you select and enter are the *Magic Search Words.*

It's a remarkable book really; the search string technique described here empowers you to get more valuable, relevant, and immediately useful information off the Internet than any other search engine tool ever created.

Search strings are a breakthrough in getting the best and most relevant information as quick as a click. They work and they can help you get results.

You will do best if you know what you want and learn the technical language of your chosen area of interest.

If you don't yet know what you want, that's OK. You'll have plenty of opportunity to find out and there are plenty of things to look at and experience. Eventually, after learning how to search, you'll want to step back and take a breather.

Use this time wisely. Plan your approach and prepare your tools. Have your off line letters, applications, letters of recommendation and references available and ready to be adapted for your use.

Then follow the steps: Search, Find, Match and Apply. These simple strategies, tactics and magic words will cut through the clutter and get you right to what you need and want the most.

Most people read through this book quickly one time. Then they go back and read it again, doing the recommended searches, to gain solid experience and knowledge. Then, you can begin to fly.

Acknowledgments

I wish to acknowledge with the deepest possible respect and thanks my parents, Helene and Murray Krupin, who gave me the most profound gift anyone can ever receive, the love of learning. My grandmother, Ida Sokol, still serves as a stalwart rock of strength and inspiration, her business sense, spiritual devotion, and dedication to finding satisfaction in service to others has shaped my own destiny into a satisfying life of public service. Working next to you as a child and a teenager Aunt Cookie, you taught me the first magic words "Can I help you". Aunt Judy, thank you for being a first class librarian and a critical reviewer with a superb eye for detail. Uncle Jack and Aunt Priscilla, thanks for sitting me down, helping me in time of need, and telling me in no uncertain terms that I have a duty to get back to business. To my family, your love, counsel, words, thoughts and feelings, conveyed to me throughout my youth, allowed the sparks of creativity to grow into a firestorm, and have helped me dedicate, channel and focus my energy towards the creation of tools that can be used to better humankind.

To my numerous colleagues in government and industry, I recognize your talents and skills and it is with great pleasure I now seek to share some of the energy, expertise, and talent you have imparted to me. Being around you and watching you work in managing the government has been a galvanizing and adventurous experience. Watching you tackle the problems of society with the tools and technologies available to us has infected me with a sense of responsibility for humanity. Thank you for allowing me to be a contributor. Your mentoring has helped motivate and shape the creation of the tools contained in these books.

Ben Kaplan, I want to say thank you for identifying the need for this book. Your own efforts, writings, enthusiasm and success motivated me to strive to create these tactics and once the ideas were conceived, to follow your lead and share them with others so they may benefit.

Dan Poynter, self publishing guru and mentor extraordinaire, you once again have shaped the world by inspiring creativity and helping a self-published author through the gauntlet to publishing success. Thank you!

Barry Kerrigan and Del LeMond, you guys are capable of much more than just Desktop Miracles, you are true alchemists, magicians of the printed word and graphic arts. I also want to thank computer wiz Tony Dolman, of Networks Northwest for keeping my computers humming and recognize the extraordinary talents and programming skills of Don Short of One World Telecommunications, without whom none of this would be possible. To Kathleen Stidham, thank you for your timely review and insights.

To agent Jeff Herman, thank you for trying! To the dozen or so east coast publishers who rejected the first version of this book, thank you! If you hadn't rejected the original manuscripts, the techniques and tactics contained in the present version of the *Magic Search Words* series would not have been created.

To my editors, Judith Whitehead, the mystery editor in New York, Angela K. Durden, and Meryl K. Evans, thank you for your hurricane force creativity and talents. Yes, I am a once-upon-a-time lawyer who still types with two fingers, thankfully knows when to ask for help, and hopefully knows how to graciously receive it. You have tactfully and elegantly guided me through the collaborative process and helped me create this incredible tool for educating and helping people with simplicity, brevity and style. Your comments and insights have helped redefine and reinvent the concepts in this book series again and again. Here's to many more happy revisions!

Most important of all, to my wife Nancy, and my two dynamite daughters, you provide me with support and inspire me to achieve. May I continue to make you proud.

PAUL KRUPIN
KENNEWICK, WASHINGTON 2002

one

Introduction

Overview

The Magic Search Word books present you with an entirely new set of easy-to-learn Internet search skills and techniques. You can use these to increase your knowledge, skills, financial success, health, and the overall quality of your life, as well as those around you.

These powerful books are written with a user view at their core. They show you exactly how to search the Internet and find the best scholarship information available quicker, faster and easier than you ever imagined possible.

You will be amazed, even if you think you know everything there is to know about the Internet. You are about to learn that there is a whole new universe at your fingertips. So be open and get ready to learn some very simple, yet mind-boggling and powerful techniques.

These books teach you how to use magic search words, create "search strings", and use special techniques like the search word rotation, the minus .com trick, searching with phrases or concepts, with personal, social of family information, or by subject, sources, date, location and much, much more.

These methods were developed by carefully distilling trial and error experience, analyzing the results from thousands and thousands of individual searches and by seeking ways to leverage the ever-improving Internet and search engine technologies.

They have been reviewed and endorsed by experts in the field of library science as well as by subject matter experts in the various topics addressed by each book.

And they deliver. You can find what you want. As quick as a click!

We encourage you to read these books carefully and then get on line and search. Use Magic Search Word techniques frequently so that you fully benefit from the powerful knowledge contained on the Internet.

We hope that you will use what you learn so that *you* may profit personally. Then, please share your newly found knowledge, skills, capability and experience with others so that they might profit as well.

Purpose

This book is all about using search engines to find and apply for scholarships.

You can quickly find the good stuff on the Internet if you learn how to do three things:

1. how to use search engines;
2. how to select the right search words; and
3. how to string the words together to do an effective search.

The key to being successful is using what I call Internet "search strings."

A search string is simply a series or *a string of key words* that you enter into the search engine to find what you are looking for. It can be two words, four words, six words or even ten or eleven words in a row.

Once you learn how to create search strings, there is no bit of information that you can't find.

To understand the power of the string search, you have to understand the paradox of the Internet. The amount of really incredible information of real value on the Internet has exploded.

From 1998 to 2001 government agencies, universities, professional organizations, and companies went online in a really big way. They keep putting more information, better information and higher quality information online every day.

While the information available was exploding, the search engines were also getting easier to use. Technology has made it quicker and easier to reach out and grab that information. Every day brings new advances. Computers are faster, plus Internet connections are better than ever and continue getting better every day.

But guess what? The technology is changing so fast that most people haven't yet come to grips with the human factors involved in taking advantage of these newly developed powers.

So much has changed that no one really knows what's out there any more. There is so much information floating out there in cyberspace, yet no one seems to know how to find the good stuff—the real gold—*information*. Information is power. It is an unfortunate paradox; we're all dressed up, we know where we want to go, but we have no idea how to get there!

Enter "Magic Search Words" and "the search string technique." These are simple and easy-to-learn methods that you can use to improve what you get off the Internet. Magic search words and the string search technique will enable you to tap into the power of the Internet like never before.

These techniques can be applied to anything. Once you learn how to use magic search words and create your own search strings, you will be able to search for information and find new opportunities easier than you ever imagined possible. It will become a tool that you incorporate into your every day pursuits for the rest of your life.

And best of all—it won't be hard to learn at all. Are you ready? Let's get started.

Getting Started

You are searching the Internet, so you will obviously need a computer with access to the Internet, a printer, and the fastest Internet connection you can find. The faster the service, the less time you have to sit and stare at the computer screen while your searches are executed.

Software is also important. You will need to be able to browse or surf the Internet using the best available software you can find. The browsing software should have come on your computer, whether you use a PC or Mac, or you can get the browser and periodic updates when you sign up for Internet access.

To make sure that you have the newest browser available, download the updates directly from the Internet. The two biggest names out there right now are Microsoft Internet Explorer and Netscape Navigator with Opera and Mozilla gaining on them. You can download these for free.

Your computer is ground zero. The most important thing to do here is learn how to use your software and use it efficiently. Part of this is trial and error, but some of it is as simple as finding the "help" button and reading the frequently asked questions (FAQ) or other helpful information that is invariably tucked away in there.

What you will want to do with the browser that you are using is create a series of bookmarks or favorite folders, and a series of sub-folders or directories.

Once you have determined what search engine you like the best, you can:

- set the browser window to default to your favorite search engine whenever you start up your Internet browser; or
- create a shortcut to your favorite search engine and place it on your desktop so that you can open your favorite search engine with one click.

How to Use This Book

In this book, you will be learning how to conduct your own custom searches. To help you learn and master the techniques, you will conduct numerous searches one at a time.

*We will tell you what words to enter by underlining the
actual search words to enter on your computer screen like this:*

<u>Search engines</u>

All you have to do go to your favorite search engine, enter the words and click.

My favorite true search engine is Google. You can get to it by opening up your Internet browser and by entering the words

www.google.com

Try it. You can, of course, use your favorite search engine or any of the other types of search engines, directories or databases that strike your fancy.

You will get to use many of these other types of search engines as you learn more about searching using this book.

Most people read through this book quickly one time. Then they go back and read it again, doing many of the recommended searches, to gain solid searching experience and knowledge.

Then, they do a self-assessment, making lists of the areas that interest and apply specifically to them. Take some time to get familiar with scholarships in general, and learn about how to create great applications.

Then, you will be ready to embark on a systematic search to identify and apply for the opportunities you discover. If you learn the techniques and implement them faithfully, you will be successful.

Free! Access to www.MagicSearchWords.com

Each of the Magic Search Words books provides you with free access to the custom programmed Magic Search Words web site.

MagicSearchWords.com automates the creation of search strings, so that creating search strings and submitting them to the best search engines is even faster and easier than ever.

You may go to www.MagicSearchWords.com anytime once you have purchased or downloaded a book.

Thank you for your interest in improving your life!

QUICKSTART
Go to www.Google.com.

CREATE A SEARCH STRING

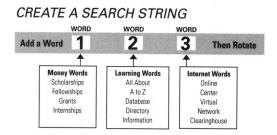

Select one word from each column and create a search string like this:

Grants A to Z Online

Then search on the words you selected. Study the results. Surf through the web sites you find and learn what they have to offer. Enjoy what you find.

Then create another search string using different words and search again.

two

All About Search Engines

There are several different types of search engines on the Internet. You will search better if you learn about them and how they work.

True Search Engines

A search engine is a Web site that is home to a specialized software program that helps you find relevant information.

"True" search engines do not search the Internet every time you enter a search term. The search engine program visits Web sites all over the Internet every so often, say once a month, and creates what is called an "index," a big vast snapshot of the pages it has visited.

When you enter a search word, the program then searches out all references to that search word in the index of the web sites it has visited. If it finds the search word, it brings back the Web site address, the universal resource locator, or URL for short.

True search engines include Google.com, Hotbot.com, Infoseek.com, and AltaVista.com. Each of these big automated search engines has four basic parts:

1. A "robot" or "spider" of some sort that automatically collects links, titles, and text from Internet sites at a certain frequency established by the people who own and manage the engine.

   What this means is that each search engine is using its own specific set of criteria to decide what kinds of information to include in its database, so each search engine you use can bring back different kinds of information, even when you use the exact same search terms.

2. A database where the collected information is stored and maintained. All the information that the spiders or robots bring back is dumped into a database from which your queries will be drawn. The more frequently the spiders are sent out, the fresher the information in the database will be.

3. An index where the collected information is cataloged for queries and retrieval. The people who own and manage the engine also establish the index. So, when you enter search terms the search engine will give you results that are listed according to the particular engine's own ranking system. Using the same search terms, each search engine can bring up a slightly different list of results because each uses a different set of criteria to determine the ranking or relevance of sites.

4. A search tool that allows the user to ask the database index for relevant sites.

Thus, when you do a search at a search engine, you actually do not search the Web, but rather you query the search engine's index of the Web. Using its index saves you time and makes the search process manageable.

All indexes collect large numbers of links, and this is both a benefit and a problem.

On the plus side, a large number of Web sites will be identified when you do a search. This will give you a complete set of data on what is out there on the Internet.

On the down side, it is very difficult to read through all the Web sites returned, and many, many of them will have little or no true relevance to your search.

True Search Engines:

All the Web
Alta Vista
Excite
Go
Google
Hotbot
Iwon
Lycos
Magellan
Teoma
Vivisimo (clustering tool)
WebCrawler

Web Directories

A Web directory is completely different than a true search engine. It is an Internet site that contains information that has been examined and categorized in a directory.

A machine creates some directory sites, while one or more human beings create the vast majority.

Instead of sending out spiders, a Web directory uses people to review and index sites using a rigid set of criteria for deciding what sites to include and exclude from the directory. These people not only look at content, but also at the quality of the site and the user experience. This is a manpower and time-consuming process and means that a Web directory will contain fewer sites than a search engine, although the sites and links are, arguably, of a better quality.

Another distinguishing feature is that a typical directory site allows you to browse through a tree of categories, sub-categories, sub-sub-categories, etc. With a search engine, you need to actually search, using either individual terms or search strings; you cannot simply click around.

Directories allow you to do just that—find things by clicking around and seeing what there is to see.

Yahoo, Netscape, and MSN are directories. Yahoo, Magellan, and Galaxy are large collections of categorized Internet sites and documents organized according to some intelligent and easy to navigate scheme.

About.com is a directory maintained by experts, called editors. About.com competitively hires over 700 expert editors, each of whom maintains the quality and content of each section of this directory.

Directories:

About.com
Britannica
LookSmart
NBCi (formerly SNAP)
Netscape
Microsoft Network (MSN)
Open Directory
Yahoo

Virtual Libraries

Numerous government agencies and universities house highly technical computerized catalog systems that are extremely large called *Virtual Libraries*. The Library of Congress hosts one of the largest in the United States. Originally, CERN created the 3W Virtual Library, in Switzerland, but it is now maintained by a consortium of institutions, including MIT.

If you search on the words "virtual libraries" you find a huge number of specialized cataloging systems for everything from microbiology to legal documents.

Meta-Search Engines

These are highly user-friendly Web sites that allow you to simultaneously send a single query to multiple search engines, directories, or specialized databases.

The Meta-Search Engine will then retrieve, combine, organize, and evaluate the results, often eliminating the duplicates, and ranking the reliability of the combined results. Some bring back all the results in one list; some let you see each source search engines results individually.

Meta-search Engines (or Multi-search Engines)

Ask Jeeves
Cyber 411
Chubba
Dogpile
Inference Fund
Mamma
MetaCrawler
MetaFind
One2Seek
Savvy Search (Savvy)

The Invisible Web

Nowadays specialized search engines, virtual libraries, and databases are all over the Web. Search engine programming and software has become readily available, and people use these technologies to entice people to visit their Web sites for the valuable information that is kept there.

Specialized search databases are often not indexed by search engine spiders. This is called the *invisible Web*.

How do you access this invisible information? Do a search!

Create your search string using the key, magic words:

invisible Web
invisible Web tutorial

Do these searches one at a time. Read the results on the Web pages that strike your fancy.

Learn about the incredible and vast amount of valuable information that is hidden from the search engines.

Search Engine Resources

One of the easiest ways to find out what search engines, directories, and software are out there is to go to a major engine you recognize or like, type in the words "search engines" and see what results are listed.

There are many sites that will explain all these searching tools in detail, list links, and point you in the right direction if you are looking for something in particular.

For quick reference, here is a summary list of some of the most powerful search strings you can use to get current and accurate information about search engines and the most popular sites:

search engines
search engine watch
search engine showdown
search engine comparison chart

Do these searches and learn as much as you want about search engines. You will learn that there are several types of search engines to choose from:

Major search engines include the most popular or important services from all over the world. They are generally commercial sites that are well maintained, and many will contain both search engines and directories you can browse.

Paid listings search engines where listings are bought and sold (*e.g.,*companies pay to be high on the return search list).

Reward search engines offer cash, prizes, or other goodies to those who use them.

News search engines search for the latest news stories from carefully selected media information sources on the Web. These services can provide exceptionally good results for current event searching because they will spider only the news sites once or twice a day. Thus, the results are unusually focused and up-to-date.

Specialty search engines are available to help you find more than just Web pages and Web sites. Here are search engines that will search through specialized search engines, newsgroups, directories, specialized search databases, mailing lists, software catalogs, and more.

Kids search engines are usually more like "safe havens, " directories maintained by people who carefully select sites to serve the beneficial interests of children. They cover things that kids really enjoy and they carefully exclude sites that parents and teachers might find inappropriate for kids, such as those that deal with explicit sexual matters, pornography, violence, hate speech, gambling, and drug use.

Metacrawlers allow searches to be sent to several search engines all at once. The results are then combined and returned on one or more pages for convenient viewing, with duplicates eliminated, ranked in order of importance, or by relevance, with regard to your search string.

Desktop search utilities are software programs that let you search the Internet from your desktop.

QUICKSTART
Go to www.Google.com.

CREATE A SEARCH STRING

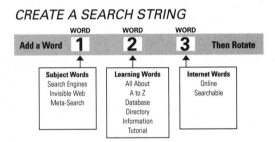

Select one word from each column and create a search string like this:

Search Engines Tutorial
Search Engines Directory
Invisible web tutorial
Invisible web online database

Then search on the words you selected. Study the results. Surf. Learn and enjoy what you find.

Then create another search string using different words and search again.

three

Magic Search Words

Most people don't know how to use a search engine. They typically use only one or two words. This yields very generalized, broad level information and often disappointing and frustrating results.

However, it doesn't have to be this way.

You get much, much better results, if you use more words. In fact, if you use a carefully selected series or string of words, it can be magic.

The Search String Technique

Simple Searches

A simple search contains one or two words.

A "search string" is a series of words that you enter into a search engine. There is a first word, then a second word, then a third word, and so on.

<u>Word # 1 Word # 2 Word # 3 Word # 4 etc . . .</u>

You can put in any series of words. You select the words to match the information you are looking for and want. Search strings contain the necessary words to find the Web site you need.

Remember, each time you add a word, the search engine looks through its database of indexed pages for Web sites that contain the words you have listed. The more words you list, the fewer Web pages will be found.

Whenever it finds a Web page with your query word on the page, it saves the URL or Web site address and brings it back to you with a list of pages where the word was found. The search engine actually brings back all the pages with your search word, sorted according to the Web site's criteria for *relevance.*

Each site's owner determines relevance by using factors such as word frequency, location of the search terms, relational clustering, link popularity, and good old pay-for-placement ranking. Generally, the more times the search word occurs, the higher on the list the Web page will be placed on the list. Voila!

A complex search, or a search string (which you will learn more about in a few pages), contains three, seven, perhaps as many as eleven carefully selected words.

Advanced Searches

Advanced searches use special terms (called Boolean terms or operators) to help you string together words to form a complex query and bring you back relevant results.

The most important advanced search terms are AND, OR, and AND NOT.

It is important to read the instructions at any search engine you use. Each search engine operates according to its own set of rules. You must read the search engine instructions to understand what you will be getting when you do a search.

The default setting can be set to either AND or OR. If you search using two words with OR, the search engine brings back a lot more web pages, than if you use the word AND.

This is because a search with two words and the default set to OR returns containing either of your words on the Web site page. If the default setting is set to AND, fewer pages will likely be found because both words will have to be present.

So, if you want to get more sites on a topic, keep the search narrow, use the search term AND and don't use the search term OR.

At the time this book was written, the following default settings were in effect:

AND—Alta Vista, Excite, Fast, Google
OR—Hot Bot, Lycos, Northern Light

Many search engines allow you to substitute plus signs (+), spaces, and minus signs (–) for AND, OR, and AND NOT. Some, on the other hand, require you to use plus signs, spaces, and minus signs for AND, OR, and AND NOT.

Remember to read the instructions of the search engines you use.

There is a world of other advanced search options that various search engines use including things like:

Wild card truncations
Automatic plurals
Proximity searching
Case sensitivity

Phrase searching
Stop words
Field searching

But for all but the most sophisticated and nerdy scientific users, you won't have to use these advanced search options.

And with the most popular search engines the technology is getting so good that you don't have to use the advanced search engine options unless you want to.

> You just enter your search words
> with a space between each word.

Explore the other search engine links and sites, so you can learn about search engines. Run the same search on other search engines.

In fact, at Google.com, you can do a search and then run the same key word searches on the other major search engines with just a click.

Concept and Phrase Searching

Here, you simply turn a typical question or phrase into the actual words you use to search.

Phrase searching is very easy to use and can get you great results. Just take a simple question that you might say out loud to another person and turn it into a search string.

One powerful technique is to take a common phrase and add it to a *<Money Word>* like the word Scholarships like this:

tips for applying for scholarships

Run your search and evaluate your results.

Next, select a different phrase with your key search word, and search again, then evaluate results. You can continue until you achieve the information and understanding you are looking for on a specific subject.

The Minus Dot Com Trick

When you do a search and want to get past the hype associated with commercial Web sites, add the following words to your search string:

−.com.

Use this technique and watch the number of sites returned get reduced by almost half. This command will virtually eliminate the commercial sites and leave only the organizations (.org), education sites (.edu), government sites (.gov) and military sites (.mil).

Let's show you how this is done.

Go to www.google.com and enter the word:

scholarships

The response from the search engine reveals over 2,000,000 web sites. The first few links on this one page are commercial sites that charge services for a fee.

Now, let's do the minus dot com trick. Enter the words:

<u>scholarships −.com</u>

The number of Web sites has dropped in half to just over 1,000,000 and the Web sites on the first page are from highly prestigious organizations from the US and other English speaking countries. If you click on some of these links you will find out exactly what it takes to apply for these opportunities very quickly.

So, if you don't want to read through the commercial sites, use "The Minus Dot Com Technique."

<u><subject> <topic> . . . −.com . . .</u>

Similarly you can focus and zero in on certain types of sites by adding the search term ".org" or ".edu" or ".gov" or ".mil." like this.

<u>Word # 1 Word # 2 Word # 3 *-.com .org*</u>

There is one drawback from using the −.com technique. Many, many commercial sites are created and managed by experts, who give away a ton of free, high quality, high value information.

If you don't view commercial sites, you won't see these resources. But finding these requires you to use some more magic search words.

Magic Search "Learning Words"

There are a group of magic search words I call "Learning Words" which can be added to a subject search to help you zero in on some of these exquisite Web sites. You used one of them when you searched on the words "invisible Web tutorial."

The word *"tutorial"* is a magic search word. If you go to Merriam-Webster's Dictionary Online you will find it defined as:

a paper, book, film, or computer program that provides practical information about a specific subject.

Pretty cool.

Free online tutorials produced by experts, as well as by universities, schools, government agencies are available on countless subjects of critical interest.

This one word can save you thousands and thousands of dollars in time, effort, and books.

Adding the word "tutorial" to a string of subject words can help locate expert information on nearly any topic quickly, so you can learn what you need to know to take your next steps.

Try the following searches:

<u>applying for scholarships tutorial</u>
<u>scholarships writing tutorial</u>
<u>grants writing tutorial</u>
<u>resumes writing tutorial</u>
<u>interviewing tutorial</u>

There are several other critical magic "Learning Words" you can use to find more critical information.

A to Z	Free
All About	Guide
Ask an Expert	Index
Ask the Professional	Introduction
Database	Library
Dictionaries	List
Directory	Manual

One major sub-category of *<Learning Words>* is "free" stuff.

The word "free" is, by itself, a powerful magic word. Use it as soon as you encounter information requiring payment. Add it to your search strings frequently.

You find the free stuff by searching on the following words:

Advice	Dos and don'ts
Book	E-mail consultations
Booklet	Forum
Bulletin board	Guide

Help   Strategies
Help centers   Tactics
Manual   Test
Online manual   Tips
Quiz   Tutorial
Self help

Magic Search "Internet Words"

You will open up additional doors to more valuable Web sites if you also use these words with another category of magic search words called "Internet Words."

These are the words that have developed since the Internet was created and became a uniquely commercialized advertising and marketing telecommunications medium.

The key magical "Internet Words" to use in search strings include:

Bank   Multimedia
Central   Network
Clearinghouse   Online
Gateway   Resource center
Interactive   Searchable
Learning center   Specialized
Link   Supersite
Market   Virtual

These words are often used in the name of a Web site or in the first paragraph describing the Web site. Hence, when you search with these words, they easily bring back these Web sites.

Now, combine these two techniques and see what sort of magic occurs.

Try some of the following searches:

<u>scholarship online database</u>
<u>scholarships searchable directories</u>
<u>scholarships associations searchable databases</u>

You can narrow these searches by adding a special subject or topic like this:

<subject> competitions associations searchable databases

Example:

computer science competitions associations searchable databases

You will learn more about how to select additional search terms to zero in on scholarships that are in your particular areas of interest in the next section.

A special word about the online scholarship search databases

I'm not a big fan of the monster databases, since I prefer to get people in direct contact with the actual source of information, and the actual funding source and authority.

The free online commercial scholarship databases are one of the available helpful aids to scholarship seekers. There are, however, several limitations that you should recognize:

- The data may not be current and the positions may or not actually be available.
- Not all the databases are complete and they draw their source data in various ways from various sources.
- The matching systems or search systems may not be perfect or even sophisticated.
- The databases have various strengths and weaknesses, and a wide range of technological programming capabilities.
- The databases will vary in content quantity, quality, timeliness, ease of use, speed, and relevance to your specific personal needs.
- You may have to provide personal information and register, and then be subjected to massive quantities of commercial product messages.

Special Tactics for Creating Search Strings

Creating Search Strings

We've discussed both search engines and the types of searches. At this point, your goal is to find Web sites that contain the certain types of information that will satisfy your wants and desires. Now, what is left to discuss is the "how"—how do you find these web sites?

You create a search word string (or a search string for short). You slowly and carefully string together a series of words.

Search strings contain the necessary magic search words to find the Web sites you need, and you create these search strings systematically, one word at a time.

1. ADD A WORD

Remember, a search string is a series of magic search words that you enter into a search engine. There is a first word, then a second word, then a third word, and so on.

<u>Word # 1 Word # 2 Word # 3 Word # 4</u>

You can put in any series of words. Your choice of words is based entirely on what you are looking to find.

But what words do you pick?

You pick the magic search words that will open up the best sources of information on the Internet.

This book is all about finding and applying for scholarships, so let's start right at the beginning and learn about them.

Go to www.google.com and enter the following phrases:

<u>applying for scholarships</u>
<u>finding scholarships</u>
<u>all about scholarships</u>
<u>types of scholarships</u>
<u>need based scholarships</u>
<u>merit based scholarships</u>

You can get a lot of basic information about scholarships by doing these simple phrase word searches.

2. SEARCH STRING WORD GROUPS

You start searching by selecting words that describe what you want to find. Selecting the best words and getting the best results often means experimenting with different but related words. These different but related words form the *search string word group.*

A *search string word group* contains the master key word you are interested in, as well as **synonyms**, which are words that mean the same thing, and other related words that are similar in meaning or purpose and can therefore be useful to you.

What this means is that a word or its synonyms or other similar related words are all useful magic search words that can be used to find high-value Web sites.

How do you find synonyms? You search of course. Search on the words:

<u>synonyms</u>

Or search on the related words

<u>online thesaurus</u>

You will find numerous free online sources that can be used to identify synonyms and related magic search words. You can always apply some plain old thinking and common sense. Related words will come to you quite readily whenever you ponder a challenge and need to come up with a word to embark on a search.

There are several key search string word groups that are useful for finding scholarships. These are:

<Money Words>	<Country or Culture Words>
<Job, Employment or Career Words>	<Family Words>
<Personal Characteristic Words>	<Military Words>
<Age Words>	<Education Words>
<Gender Words>	<Action Words>

<Internet Words>   <Location Words>
<Learning Words>   <Source Words>
<Industry Words>   <Media Words>
<Association Words>   <Time Words>

There are many more search string word groups you will think up as you identify and pursue your particular and unique needs. We'll talk about these again in more detail later.

When you create a search string use the "add a word" technique. Select one word from one key search string word group and then add another word from another word group and so on and so on.

You vary your word selection to meet your needs. You add words in sequence, with a specific purpose, one word at a time so that your search results bring you back results—Web pages that contain the words you seek.

Then, you evaluate the results of your search.

Obviously, this will take time. But, it will be worth your time and effort if you go through this process.

Start at the beginning with your most general search and conduct one search after the other, reading and evaluating the results along the way, as you work though a short list of the search words.

Here is an example:

Goal: Identify college scholarships for minority women interested in computer software programming in Washington state, with Microsoft, in the year 2002.

Follow along and pay careful attention as we build this search string together. Open your browser and go to your favorite search engine. Either enter what is presented below, or enter your own personal interests and information. The underlined words are the words you add at each step.

1. First you enter the magic search words that contains a *<Money Word>*.

scholarships

2. Then add an *<Education Word>*.

college scholarships

3. Add a *<Personal Characteristic Word>*.

<u>College scholarship **minority woman**</u>

4. Add an *<Educational Subject Word>*.

<u>College scholarship minority woman **computers**</u>

5. Add a *<Topic Word>*.

<u>College scholarship minority woman computers **programming**</u>

6. Add a *<Subtopic Word>*.

<u>College scholarship minority woman computers programming **software**</u>

7. Add a *<Location Word>*.

<u>College scholarship minority woman computers programming software **Washington**</u>

8. Add a *<Financial Source Word>*, in this case a specific company by name, Microsoft.

<u>College scholarship minority woman computers programming software Washington **Microsoft**</u>

9. Finally, add a *<Date Word>* to capture the most current information and eliminate outdated information.

<u>College scholarship minority woman computers programming software Washington Microsoft **2002**</u>

As you construct the search string, take a look at the list of Web sites your search brings up, step by step.

Click on a couple of the sites and see what kinds of information they contain, but don't spend too much time on each initial step. Go back to the search form page and continue to add words. Work your way through to the end and create the ten-word search string.

This table illustrates how each word is associated with a word group.

Search word	Word Group	Example
Word 1	Education Word	College
Word 2	Money Word	Scholarship
Words 3 & 4	Personal Characteristic	Minority woman
Word 5	Subject Word	Computer
Word 6	Topic Word	Programming
Word 7	Sub-topic Word	Software
Word 8	Location Word (State)	Washington
Word 9	Financial Source Word (Company by name)	Microsoft
Word 10	Date Word	2002

Wow. You nailed it. You found what you were looking for: Web sites with scholarship information for woman minority students interested in computer software programming in Washington.

For those of you reading along, assume that you have executed the search, evaluated your results by clicking on some of the more promising sites.

Now, we're going to introduce a new technique that will open up a whole new world of possibilities with just one click.

3. SEARCH WORD ROTATION

Let's say you searched on the words:

college scholarship woman computers programming software Washington Microsoft 2002

Wouldn't you love to find more similar opportunities?

What you do is simply substitute one magic search word in the search string to focus your search on those other types of opportunities.

The word "scholarships" is a *<Money Word>*, that is, it describes a form of financial aid.

Now ask yourself, "What other similar types of financial aid opportunities might I be interested in?"

Here is a short list of similar opportunities:

Fellowships	Grant programs
Internships	Grants
Assistantships	Work study
Research assistantships	Exchange programs
Teaching assistantships	Financial aid

Now use the "search word rotation" technique. What you do is rotate or substitute just one word, in this case, your key *<Money Word>* with another one of the *<Money Words>* on your list. Then, search again to find Web sites that contain these words and represent new opportunities.

You rotate the search words like this:

Search 1 = College *fellowship* woman computers programming software Washington Microsoft 2002

Search 2 = College *internship* woman computers programming software Washington Microsoft 2002

Search 3 = College *grants* woman computers programming software Washington Microsoft 2002

And so on.

This is very powerful. So take your time.

You can rotate the magic search words in your search string with synonyms or similar words for any word you select and continue to find more new and different Web sites.

One of the most powerful actions you can take is to switch from *<Money Words>* to other types of financial opportunities by using the *<Job, Employment or Career Words>* search string word group category:

Employment	Openings
Jobs	Announcements
Career	Vacancy Announcements
Positions	Volunteer
Opportunities	Titles
Work	Positions
Training	Apprentices
Vacancies	Help wanted

Remember each time you do this, rotate just one word and retain the remainder of the original string of magic search words, keeping all the other words in the search string the same. Be slow and systematic. Make only one change at a time.

This is actually a really great exercise for you to do on your computer, so you can see just how powerful a tool you now have at your fingertips.

You can use this technique to find scholarships, jobs, health information, legal advice, or just about anything.

The selective addition of words allows you to take advantage of the incredible power of search engine technology.

Each additional word opens up an entirely new, but equally detailed, set of search results. And all you did was add one word to your search.

Think of the possibilities! You can use magic search words, create all sorts of search strings, and rotate through a whole new universe of different areas of knowledge, opportunity, and interest.

Congratulations. If you use these techniques, you can now explore the realm of possibility like never before.

4. SEARCH BY EDUCATION, AGE OR GRADE LEVEL

You can select and rotate magic search words to focus on people of a certain education level, age or grade level. You use the following magic search words:

Teens	Associate
Students	Two year
Elementary school	Four year
High school	Community college
Teachers	College
Parents	University
K–6	Bachelors
K–12	Masters
Middle school	Graduate
Private school	Postgraduate
Vocational	Doctoral
Technical	Postdoctoral

5. SEARCH BY LOCATION

You can add a city, county, state, region or country to your search string and systematically search city by city through places you are interested in like this:

<u>sport scholarships</u> **Los Angeles California**
<u>sports scholarships</u> **San Diego California**
<u>sports scholarships</u> **San Francisco California**
<u>sports scholarships</u> **Miami Florida**
<u>sports scholarships</u> **Tampa Florida**

You can also search by county, region, country, province, or use national, or international words.

Geography and location can be used to effectively to pinpoint opportunities with many of the search string word groups.

6. SEARCH BY DATE

You can eliminate Web sites that are outdated by adding the current or upcoming year to your search string like this:

<u>Environmental Engineering Research Grants EPA Washington DC **2002**</u>

However, don't be too hasty in doing this. Many Web sites don't change information every year, and the inclusion of the year or date will eliminate many sites that may interest you.

7. SEARCHING FOR SPECIFIC SOURCES OF INFORMATION

You can use words that will specifically focus on the different types of organizations that offer scholarships, fellowships, internships, or sponsor competitions with various prizes or awards:

Government

City, county, state, regional, and federal government agencies

Business

Companies & corporations
Companies by name

Associations

Professional and trade associations
Professional and trade organizations
Nonprofit organizations
Philanthropic foundations, institutions

Trade groups
Fraternal organizations
Community organizations

Educational Institutions

Schools, Colleges, Universities

Each of these is a key component of the *<Financial Source Words>* word group that has specific terminology that is best used when searching the Internet. The later chapters of this book provide special techniques and magic search words and terminology to use in searching the specific sources of financial aid.

8. SEARCH THE MEDIA (PRINT AND ELECTRONIC)

Most media have Web sites on the Internet. You start by finding media on the Internet by creating a search string using the magic words Media *<Learning Words> <Internet Words>* like this:

<u>media online directory</u>
<u>media online database</u>

Next, use the add a word technique to isolate the type of media you are interested in:

Daily newspapers
Weekly newspapers
News services
News syndicates
Magazines
Trade publications
Radio
Television

Search for specific media by location either by state or city and state. Finally, once you are on a Web site for a specific media publication, search that site for the information you seek.

Media tend to have what we described earlier as "invisible Web" resources. To gain access to those resources you must first go to the

Web site, then locate the entrance to search tools. After locating the directories, searchable databases and libraries, you can follow the instructions and use the resources.

For example search on the following words:

<u>daily newspapers New York</u>

Then search for one of the newspapers you find. It could be The New York Times, The Wall Street Journal, or Newsday.

Once you get to the media's Web site, then search on the word "scholarships" along with your other topics of interest.

At newspapers and magazines you will find articles about the subjects you are interested in. At professional journals you will find peer reviewed technical articles.

More and more media organizations are going online and they will give you searchable database or directory access to their archives. Some are for free while others are accessible for a fee.

9. USE CONCEPT OR PHRASE SEARCHING

Simple Phrase Searching

Here, you turn a typical question or phrase into the actual words you use to search.

Phrase searching is easy to use and can get you great results. Just take a simple question that you might say out loud to another person and turn it into a search string.

One powerful technique is to take a common phrase and add it to a *<Money Word>*. Run your search and evaluate your results.

Select a different phrase with your *<Money Word>*, and search again, then evaluate results. You can continue till you achieve the information and understanding you are looking for on a certain subject.

The search string construction looks like this:

<u><phrase> <Money Word></u>
<u><phrase> <Money Word> <Issue Word></u>

There are lots of phrases that you can use:

An introduction to
Dealing with applications
How to prepare
Planning for
Protecting against
The best techniques for
The biggest mistakes
The role of
Best tips on
Best advice
Understanding how to

Here are some examples:

<u>managing your scholarship search</u>
<u>winning scholarship essays</u>
<u>biggest scholarship essay mistakes</u>
<u>how to fill out scholarship application forms</u>
<u>avoiding college financial aid problems</u>
<u>beware of Scholarship scams</u>
<u>scholarship databases for minorities</u>

More Detailed Phrase Searching

You can use more detailed phrase searching by adding more search string word groups to your phrase. For example, to find information to help family members, the search string construction is this:

<u><phrase> <Money Word> <Personal Relation> <Action Word></u>

You enter the phrase with the words from any other search string word groups you wish to research.

Mothers of graduating high school students
When your *<Personal Relation>* needs a *<Money Word>*
How to help your *<Family Member>* find a *<Money Word>*
Here are some examples:

<u>when your daughter needs a scholarship</u>
<u>how to help your son get a scholarship</u>
<u>dealing with specific financial aid problems</u>
<u>overcoming poor grades scholarships</u>

10. EXACT QUOTE SEARCHING

This technique is useful when you are looking for an exact book title or an article about something specific.

With some search engines you enter the exact sequence of words you want to use with quotation marks around them.

Other search engines have you enter the words in a special text box.

In any case, you should refer to and use the advanced search engine instructions that you find on the particular search engine you are using.

Here are some examples:

<u>"merit-based scholarships California"</u>
<u>"Harry S Truman scholarship program"</u>

You can also use exact quote searching to find specific companies, facilities, schools, or universities, or government agencies or professional organizations.

Examples:

<u>"American Society of Civil Engineers"</u>
<u>"Direct Marketing Association"</u>
<u>"Harvard University School of Business"</u>
<u>"National Federation of Teachers"</u>

Some search engines consider some words to be so common that they are ignored. These are typically called "stop words." If you read the advanced search engine instructions, you can find a way around this. Google, for example, will let you include a "stop word" if you place a "plus sign" in front of the stop word, like this:

<u>scholarships +in the computer industry</u>

You may get very few results by using exact quote searching, but you will likely get exactly what you asked for.

11. SEARCH FOR INFORMATION IN DIFFERENT LANGUAGES

Information is available on the Internet from a wide variety of countries all over the world, in numerous languages.

You can enter your search in the language you are seeking to find the information.

You can also enter your search in English and add the specific language you are seeking.

Example:

computer scholarships bilingual

scholarships Los Angeles Spanish

You can also search for the country you are looking for.
Example:

scholarship information South Africa

scholarship opportunities Australia

You can also search for Web sites that are located in a certain country by entering the URL country code:

overseas scholarship information France French .fr

scholarship student exchange program information Russia .ru

Find Internet country codes by conducting a search using the magic words:

Internet country codes

Some search engines allow you to select Web sites that contain the selected language you want. For example, go to www.Google.com, and select your desired language in the preferences setting.

Magic Search Words Roadmap

The following chart illustrates how to select magic search words to create search strings using the word groups discussed in the chapter.

Magic Search Words
SCHOLARSHIPS

CREATE A SEARCH STRING

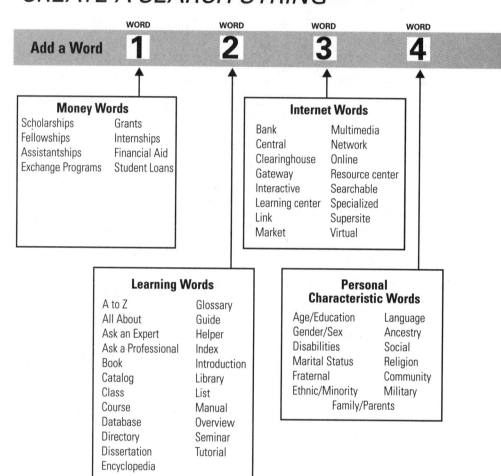

Add a Word	WORD **1**	WORD **2**	WORD **3**	WORD **4**

Money Words
Scholarships	Grants
Fellowships	Internships
Assistantships	Financial Aid
Exchange Programs	Student Loans

Internet Words
Bank	Multimedia
Central	Network
Clearinghouse	Online
Gateway	Resource center
Interactive	Searchable
Learning center	Specialized
Link	Supersite
Market	Virtual

Learning Words
A to Z	Glossary
All About	Guide
Ask an Expert	Helper
Ask a Professional	Index
Book	Introduction
Catalog	Library
Class	List
Course	Manual
Database	Overview
Directory	Seminar
Dissertation	Tutorial
Encyclopedia	

Personal Characteristic Words
Age/Education	Language
Gender/Sex	Ancestry
Disabilities	Social
Marital Status	Religion
Fraternal	Community
Ethnic/Minority	Military
Family/Parents	

Search Engines
True Search Engines   Invisible Web

Virtual Libraries   Directories   Metasearch

Concept & Phrase Searches

The Minus .com Trick
-.com

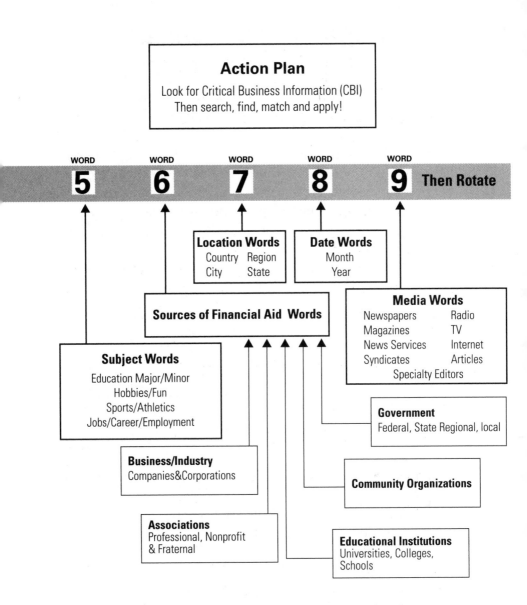

Action Plan

Look for Critical Business Information (CBI)
Then search, find, match and apply!

WORD **5** WORD **6** WORD **7** WORD **8** WORD **9** Then Rotate

Location Words
Country Region
City State

Date Words
Month
Year

Sources of Financial Aid Words

Media Words
Newspapers Radio
Magazines TV
News Services Internet
Syndicates Articles
Specialty Editors

Subject Words
Education Major/Minor
Hobbies/Fun
Sports/Athletics
Jobs/Career/Employment

Government
Federal, State Regional, local

Business/Industry
Companies&Corporations

Community Organizations

Associations
Professional, Nonprofit
& Fraternal

Educational Institutions
Universities, Colleges,
Schools

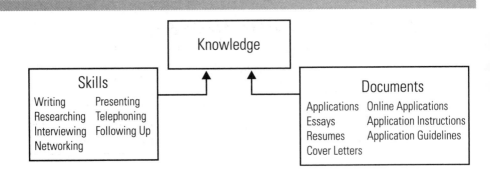

Knowledge

Skills

Writing Presenting
Researching Telephoning
Interviewing Following Up
Networking

Documents

Applications Online Applications
Essays Application Instructions
Resumes Application Guidelines
Cover Letters

Practice the basic search skills

First, open up your favorite search engine. My favorite is Google.com, but you may like another. It doesn't matter which one you like the best.

Then, read the next section looking for something that interests you.

Once you find what you are interested in, create a search string using the search words that you want to use. Keep your search strings simple and focus on one area of interest at a time to start:

<scholarships> <subject>

Then make them more targeted

<scholarships> <subject> <location>

Then use the search word rotation technique with synonyms and related words.

Search with various *<Internet Words>* and *<Learning Words>*.

Search using various *<Information Source Words>*.

Finally, switch to a new subject and start over again. For example, if you are interested in film-making internships enter the words

film-making internships

Or, if you want to find just those opportunities in Los Angeles, California enter the words

film-making internships Los Angeles California

After that, think of all the other synonyms for each key search word group and related terms and search on those, too.

Think of all the possible synonyms for the key words you are focusing on and search for those. Make sure you use the *<Internet Words>*.

We'll teach you to get more systematic and comprehensive about searching for scholarship information in the next section. For now, just play with what you've learned so far.

Got it? Now, turn on your computer.

Ready? Get set.

Go!

four

The Magic Search Words Kingdom

It is crucial to see the big picture and understand what you are doing when you search for scholarships on the Internet. You are using magic search words to search out power in the universe.

Words have magic. They lead you to information. Information gives you power. Power enables you to take action. Action allows you to realize benefits.

The better the magic search words, the better the information you find, the more powerful you will become.

Overview of the Kingdom

Work through this next section slowly and carefully to clearly understand and master how to use these procedures. You are going to learn how to select magic search words from six major realms of technology and knowledge.

Each realm contains several key search string word groups. Pay attention to how these are organized because they form a framework for searching that will become a powerful tool for you to use.

1. The Internet itself: You take advantage of the terminology and technology the Internet offers. We introduced this when we showed you all about search engines and how they work. You already know how to use the Magic Search Words for uncovering high quality educational information. These are:
   • Learning Words
   • Internet Words
2. You search for scholarships and other forms of financial aid and use the magic search words:
   • Money Words
   • Job, Employment and Career Words
3. You identify and recognize who you are and what you want, e.g., your qualifications, characteristics and interests:
   • Personal and social characteristics
   • Education and personal interests
   • Career interests
   • Industry interests
4. You search for the specific sources of financial aid:
   • Government
   • Schools
   • Professional and nonprofit associations
   • Companies and corporations
   • Community organizations
5. You adjust your search to meet other personal needs or desires:
   • Location
   • Time
6. You also search for information that will provide you with additional information and possible sources of knowledge and contacts.
   • Media

When you create search strings, the Magic Search Words you will use come from the Key Search String Word Groups contained in each of the six realms.

Magic Potions: The Key Search Word String Word Groups

This section contains a mid-level look at the types of magic search words that you can use in the actual search strings you create. The next section drops down to one more level of detail to give you even more specifics.

Three Specific Goals for Searching

You select search words to achieve three specific all-important objectives:

1. Increasing your knowledge of scholarships in general.
2. Identifying actual scholarship opportunities for which you can apply.
3. Improving your skills in applying and winning the scholarships that you find.

When you create search strings you aim at satisfying your needs in one of these areas.

You use the search string word groups to guide your selection of the right magic search words each time you do a search to achieve your objectives.

Inside the Search String Word Groups

Below each word group listed here you will find important magic search words you can use to create search strings.

Go forth and use them wisely.

<Learning Words>

A to Z

All about

Ask an expert

Ask the professional
Database
Dictionaries
Directory
Guide
Index
Introduction
Library
List
Manual
Thesaurus

<Internet Words>

Central
Clearinghouse
Interactive
Learning center
Link
Market
Multimedia
Network
Online
Resource center
Searchable
Specialized
Supersite
Virtual

<Money Words>

Scholarships
Fellowships
Internships
Assistantships
Research assistantships
Teaching assistantships
Grant programs
Grants

Work study
Exchange programs
Financial aid

<Personal Characteristic Words>

Language
Ancestry
Religion
Ethnic or minority
Age/year/education level
Gender
Family/marital status
Disability/handicap

<Social Characteristics Words>

Social characteristics
Fraternal organizations
Community organizations
Military involvement/relations

<Education and Personal Interest Words>

Personal interests
Hobbies/interests
Sports/athletics
Education
Major fields of study
Minor fields of study
Fun subjects

<Career Words>

Fields of employment
Positions
Titles
Occupations
Vocations
Industry

<Industry Words>

Industry by name
Categories by subject
Organizations by title
Companies by name

<Government Words>

Government agencies
Type
Source
Subject
Category
Classification
Function
Branch
Geography

<Business Words>

Companies
Corporations
Type
Source
Subject
Category
Industry
Location
Actual name
News
Media
Organizations
Personnel

<Associations and Organization Words>

Associations
Organizations

Type
Profit
Nonprofit
Source
Subject
Industry
Geography
Actual name
Personnel

<Geography and Location Words>

Specific location
Continent
Abroad
Country
State
Province
Region
County
City

<Time Words>

Time
Year
Month
Day
Deadline
Date

<Media Words>

Media
Media categories
Editors
Reporters
Columnists
Correspondents

Magic Spells: Selecting the Magic Search Words

This section gives you the more detailed insider's view of the search string word groups. At this level, you will have the greatest success in selecting magic search words. Let's look closely at each of the search string word groups and how to best make use of magic search words contained in them.

Using the Money Words

Use the word "scholarship" as the first word in your search string.

Add any and all the other words you select from specific search word groups to these money words like this:

<Money Words> plus the rest of your search string.

Then use the search word rotation with synonyms or similar words.

The money words:

Scholarships
Fellowships
Internships
Assistantships
Research assistantships
Teaching assistantships
Grant programs
Work study
Exchange programs
Financial aid

Use *<Money Words>* one at a time in a single search.

Then, use the search word rotation technique.

Improving Your Knowledge in General

Use the *<Money Words>* to increase your knowledge of scholarships in general. Couple them with *<Learning Words>* and *<Internet Words>* to get started and begin your quest for knowledge.

You can use the search word rotation technique to broaden your knowledge and increase your understanding of various aspects of your objectives.

Phrase and concept searching is also a helpful tool to use. You use simple oral statements or questions to frame your search string. You can also use phrases you find in other literature, articles, or in some of the search results you discover along the way.

Examples:

<u>guide to scholarships</u>
<u>financial aid information guide</u>
<u>parents searching for scholarships</u>

You use the *<Money Words>* with the *<Learning Words>* and *<Internet Words>* to get started. Then use the search word rotation technique to broaden your knowledge.

Identifying Actual Scholarship Opportunities

To identify actual scholarship opportunities, for which you can apply, use the *<Money Words>* with other search string word groups to define your specific goal or target.

<u><scholarships> <personal interest> <sources of financial aid> <location> <date></u>

Example:

<u>scholarships sports universities Georgia 2002</u>

This looks simple, but actually this is where there is a lot of work to be done.

You create search strings based on your first area of interest.

Next, systematically rotate through the *<Money Words>* search word group.

Then go back to your first *<Money Word>* and do it all over again this time rotating on the *<Personal Interest Words>*.

Then you should look start over again and search through one *<source of financial aid>* at a time. Then try the search word rotation technique to search in other sources of financial aid.

If you do this slowly and systematically, you will discover more opportunities than you ever imagined. You will identify many, many new opportunities you never knew existed.

Improving your skills in applying and writing

To improve your skills in applying for and winning those scholarships you find, use the *<Money Words>* with a *<Learning Word>*, a specific *<Document Word>* and a specific *<Skill Word>* you are interested in.

Example:

<u>scholarship essays writing tutorial</u>

<Document Words>

Applications
Essays
Resumes
Cover Letters
Online Applications
Application Instructions
Application Guidelines

<Skill Words>

Writing
Researching
Interviewing
Networking
Presenting
Telephoning
Following Up

Using the job and employment words

Use a word *<Job, Employment or Career Word>* as the first word in your search string, as an alternative to using a *<Money Word>*.

Employment	Vacancies
Jobs	Openings
Career	Announcements
Positions	Volunteer
Opportunities	Titles
Help wanted	Positions
Positions available	Apprentices
Openings	Intern
Work	Mentor
Training	Assistant

Add any and all the other words you select from specific search word groups to these money words like this:

<Job, Employment or Career Word> plus the rest of your search string.

Use the search word rotation with synonyms or similar words.

You can use the *<Job, Career and Employment Words>* the same way you use the *<Money Words>* to improve your general knowledge, identify specific opportunities, or improve your application skills.

Using *<Money Words>* and *<Job, Career and Employment Words>* gives you extremely powerful tools to pursue your life goals.

Using the financial aid source words

You must focus your searches on high potential sources of financial aid. Do this by using the *<Financial Aid Source Words>* in your search string.

<u>\<Money Words\> \<Source Word\></u>

The financial aid source words include terms associated with the entire spectrum of government agencies, businesses, companies, corporations large and small, professional associations, nonprofit organizations, and universities, colleges, and other educational institutions.

For example:

<u>scholarship information professional associations</u>
<u>scholarship information government</u>
<u>scholarship information foundations</u>

Use these one at a time and rotate through them. Use the *<Source words>* with the *<Money Words>* to improve your general knowledge, identify specific opportunities, or improve your application skills.

You will find that many of the source organizations provide excellent educational and scholarship search resources.

Using location and date words

Use location and date words at the end of your search string.

<u><Money Words> <Source Word> <Location Words> <Date Words></u>

For example:

<u>scholarship information government California 2002</u>
<u>scholarship information universities California 2002</u>

Use *<Location Words>* one at a time and rotate through them.

You can use *<Location Words>* with the *<Money Words>* and *<Source Words>* to find ways to improve your general knowledge at institutions in the areas in which you are interested.

Also try *<Location Words>* and *<Date Words>* to identify specific, current opportunities or to improve your application skills at the places in your area of choice.

CREATE A SEARCH STRING

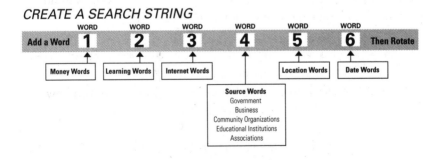

CHAPTER

five

Make a Wish and Cast a Spell

To be successful in your search you must know who you are, what you want, where you want to go, and when you want to be there.

Focus on what you like and enjoy doing the most. School and education should be enjoyable. The work or career you choose should be something that makes you happy. Do what you love.

Be specific and careful about what you wish for. You may get exactly what you asked for—exactly what you want. Create your search strings using the magic words.

Cast your spell by describing: what, who, where, when, and how.

Decide What You Want

The first step in creating your search string is to identify exactly what you are looking for. Be specific.

The first search word of your search string should always be a
<Money Words> like:

Scholarship
Fellowships
Internships
And so on. . . .

The words you select should come from the lists of *<Money Words>*
or *<Job, Career and Employment Words>*.

Identify Who You Are

Next, focus on your personal, social or cultural characteristics or "special qualifications."

You may be one of those people who will qualify for specific
opportunities because of some relatively unique or special personal,
social, or cultural characteristics (e.g., women, minorities, religion,
military, disabilities).

Identify them. Make a list of every identifiable personal, social or
cultural characteristic that may qualify you for a financial opportunity.

Once you identify these characteristics, you must use them as
magic search words. You will search for them specifically and use
them in your search string. Then, the search string will focus on one
or more of the following special qualifications:

- Personal, social & cultural characteristics
- Key areas of interest (hobbies, interests, sports, etc.)
- Education—Major/minor fields of study
- Age (year, or group, e.g. K–12, 9–12)
- School year (high school, college, graduate)
- Religion, ethnic or ancestry

WHY IS THIS IMPORTANT?

Each and every one of the personal or social characteristics
becomes a possible search term for you to use as you search for financial aid opportunities.

These characteristics are important because money is specifically available for people with specific interests or characteristics.

Use these words in your search strings to help you identify and connect you with certain opportunities where these factors give you an advantage or form a critical element of what is acceptable to you.

Specifically, if you have certain personal qualities, you may find that these qualify you for special scholarships or other financial aid opportunities. For example, there are special scholarships available to minority or economically disadvantaged individuals.

There are scholarship opportunities available for every other identified personal, cultural or special characteristic or qualification. All you need to do is search for them.

These are your special characteristics, qualifications, interests, capabilities and assets. Take advantage of what you are. Use them.

PERSONAL CHARACTERISTICS

Identify your personal, social and other distinctive cultural characteristics. Include your family and close relations. Be prepared to use your personal, social and other distinctive characteristics to your advantage. These may represent unique opportunities you can leverage at some point in your search.

<Language>

English
Chinese
French
German
Italian
Japanese
Russian
Spanish
Swahili

<Ancestry>

African
American Indian

Arapaho Tribe
Armenian
Blackfeet
Cambodian
Canadian
Cherokee
Cheyenne
Chinese
Choctaw
Cuban
Cypriot
Danish
Filipino
Finnish

Greek
Hawaiian
Hopi
Hualapai
Huguenot
India
Italian
Japanese
Jewish
Korean
Laotian
Lithuanian
Mexican/Hispanic
Miccosukee
Mongolian
Native Hawaiian
Navajo
Norwegian
Oneida
Pacific Islander
Polish
Portuguese
Puerto Rican
Russian
Scandinavian
Scottish
Seminole
Seneca
Serbian
Shoshone
Singaporean
Soviet
Spanish
Swedish
Swiss
Thai
Vietnamese

Welsh

\<Religion\>

Atheist
Agnostic
Bahai
Baptist
Brethren
Catholic
Christian
Christian Science
Christian Church
Eastern Orthodox
Jewish
Lutheran
Muslim
Presbyterian
Sikh
Unitarian
United Church of Christ
United Methodist Church

\<Ethnic or Minority\>

Afro-American
American Indian
Native American Indian
Eskimo
Arab
Asian
Hispanic
Puerto Rican
Hindu
Oriental
Middle Eastern

\<Age\>

Baby

Infant
Child
Teen
Youth
Young Adult
Mature
Senior Citizen
Elderly

\<Year/Education Level>

K–6
K–12
Teens
9th grade
10th grade
11th grade
12th grade
Elementary
Elementary school
Middle school
High school
Associate
Baccalaureate
Bachelors
College
Community college
Two Year
Four year
Freshman
Junior
Sophomore
Senior
Graduate
Masters
Parents
Private school
Secondary

Students
Teachers
Technical
Doctoral
Postdoctoral
Postgraduate
University
Vocational

\<Gender>

Male
Female
Boy
Girl
Man
Woman

\<Family/Marital Status>

Single
Married
Parent
Single parent with child
Unmarried parent
Divorced
Widowed

\<Disability/Handicap>

Amputee
Asthma
Attention Deficit Disorder
Blind
Cooley's Anemia
Deaf
Dyslexia
Economic
Epilepsy
Hearing Impaired

Hemophilia / Bleeding Disorder
Learning Disability
Minority
Paraplegic

Speech Impaired
Visually Impaired
Wheelchair confined

<Fraternal Organizations>

Identify and search on any fraternal organizations that you or any of your family members may be involved in.

Fraternities
Sororities
Brotherhoods
Sisterhoods

Examples:

Delta Gamma Sorority
Rotary
Knights of Pythias
Knights of Columbus
Lions Club

<Community Organizations>

Identify any involvement, participation, or volunteerism in organizations and activities you are involved in or have contributed to, or activities members of your family have been involved in. Search for scholarships with these organizations. Get your relative to sponsor you or give you a letter of recommendation or introduction.

<Military Involvement / Relations>

Identify any organizations and activities you are involved in or have contributed to, or members of your family are or have been involved in.

Examples:

Army
Navy
Marines

Reserve
Air Force

Identify What You Are Interested in

Instead of a personal or social characteristic, you may want to identify opportunities associated with your particular area of interest.

Identify these subjects and use them as magic search words in your search strings.

PERSONAL INTERESTS, SPORTS, AND EDUCATION

Identify your key areas of interest. Make a list of the things that you enjoy and love to do. Use these words as magic search words.

Personal interests
Hobbies
Sports
Education
Major fields of study
Minor fields of study
Fun subjects

<Hobbies / Interests>

Aviation/flying
Birds
Caddies/golf
Cats
Coins
Cows
Diving
Dogs
Fishing
Gardening
Ham radio
Harness racing
Horses
Hunting

Quilting
Sewing
Skating
Soccer
Stamps
Swimming

<Sports/Athletics>

Aerobics
Baseball
Basketball
Dance
Football
Gymnastics
Martial Arts
Skiing
Soccer
Softball
Swimming
Tennis
Track
Volleyball
Water sports

<Education>

Identify the fields of education that interest you—get familiar with the options and many various activities and research the various fields offer. Learn what people who get educated in these fields do and where they go. You may be surprised at how many areas of application make use of specific disciplines and technologies. Identify and search for scholarships within your:

<Major fields of study>
<Minor fields of study>
<All other educational subjects you take>

Use the following list to help you identify the field(s) you may be interested in studying.

Be systematic. Make a list of the courses that you like and enjoy. Use these as magic search words in your search strings.

Agriculture

Agribusiness
Agricultural economics
Agricultural engineering /
    mechanics
Agricultural marketing
Agricultural production / technology
Agronomy / crop science
Animal science
Dairy science
Equine studies
Farm management
Floriculture
Golf grounds management
Herb studies
Horticulture
Pomology
Poultry science
Range management
Soil science
Turf/grounds management
Turfgrass science

Art

Animation
Art administration/management
Art conservation
Art history
Cartooning
Ceramic arts
Commercial art
Crafts
Design
Drawing
Fashion design
Film and video
Fine arts
Graphic arts
Interior design
Multimedia
Museum education
Numismatics
Painting
Photography
Printing

Printmaking
Sculpture
Textile design
Visual arts

Biological Sciences

Astrobiology
Biology
Biophysics
Biospace
Biotechnology
Botany
Ecology
Cellular biology
Conservation
Dendrology
Developmental biology
Ecology
Endocrinology
Enology / viticulture
Entomology
Environmental economics
Environmental education
Environmental epidemiology
Environmental health
Environmental radioactivity
Environmental science
Evolutionary biology
Fisheries
Forestry
Game
Genetics
Health physics
Herpetology
Lakes
Limnology

Marine Biology
Marine science
Microbiology
Molecular biology
Neurobiology
Ornithology
Physiology
Pollution control
Recreation
Riparian area management
Riverine
Tree science
Virology
Water resources management
Watershed management
Wilderness area management
Wildlife
Wildlife conservation
Zoology

Business

Administration
Accounting
Actuarial science
Advertising
Art administration
Aviation management
Airport management
Banking
Business ethics
Club management
Cost estimation
Data processing
Economics
Finance
Garden center management

Golf course management
Grocery industry
Hotel administration
Industrial and labor relations
Information systems
Insurance
Integrated resource management
International business
Labor studies
Human resources
Management
Manufacturing
Marketing
Merchandising
Operations research
Production / operations
    management
Public administration
Public relations
Real estate
Real estate appraising
Recreation / resource management
Restaurant management
Retail management
Sports management
Traffic management
Transportation
Travel and tourism
Youth/human service agency
    administration

Chemistry

Atmospheric chemistry
Biochemistry
Chemical technology
Geochemistry

Communications

Broadcasting
Electronic media
Financial / business journalism
Home workshop writing
Journalism
News editing
News graphics
Newspaper business
Photojournalism
Print journalism
Print media
Printing
Public relations
Public sector
Publishing
Religious
Sports
Technical writing
Telecommunications
Television
Video

Computers

Computer programming
Computer hardware
Software

Earth Science

Astronomy
Astrophysics
Cartography
Cave research
Climatology
Conservation
Ecology

Energy
Environmental economics
Environmental education
Environmental epidemiology
Environmental health
Environmental radioactivity
Environmental science
Fisheries
Game
Geodetic surveying
Geography
Geology
Geophysics
Geosciences
Health physics
Hydrology
Hydrogeology
Lakes
Land use
Land use planning
Limnology
Marine biology
Marine science
Marine technology
Materials science and engineering
Meteorology
Mineral economics
Mineralogy
Oceanography
Pollution control
Recreation
Remote sensing
Riparian area management
Riverine
Water resources management
Watershed management
Wilderness area management

Wildlife

Education

Administration / management
Blind / visually impaired
Child care
Christian leadership
Deaf / hearing impaired
Early childhood
Elementary
English as a second language
Gifted / talented
Health
Learning disabled
Library
Media
Music
Orientation/mobility
Physical
Post-secondary
Reading
School library
Science
Special
Speech
Technology
Vocational
Youth leadership

Engineering, General

Aeronautics
Aerodynamics
Aeronautical engineering
Aerospace history
Aerospace technology
Astronautics

Space science

Vertical flight

Architecture

Architectural engineering
Architectural history
Design arts
Environmental design
Health facilities
Landscape architecture
Naval architecture
Urban planning

Aviation

Aviation
Aviation electronics
Aviation writing
Aviation/aerospace history
Chemical engineering
Civil engineering
Construction
Public works administration
Structural engineering

Computer science

Artificial intelligence
Communications
Computer graphics
Computer programming
Computer systems
Electrical engineering
Electronics
Microelectronics
Vacuum science

Environmental engineering

Geological engineering
Hydraulic engineering

Industrial engineering
Industrial hygiene
Nuclear engineering
Optical engineering

Technical engineering

Arc welding technology
Audio production
Automotive technology
Die casting technology
Heating, refrigeration, & air-
    conditioning
Lubrication / tribology engineering
Manufacturing technology /
    engineering
Photographic / imaging science
Plumbing
Power generation
Pulp and paper technology
Radar
Remote sensing
Robotics
Satellites

Mechanical engineering

Material science
Metallurgy
Mining engineering
Naval science
Navigation
Petroleum engineering
Sanitary engineering

English language / literature

British literature
Classics
Creative writing
Debate forensics

Folklore
Library science
Library science—law
Linguistics
Literature
Oratory
Playwriting
Poetry
Reading / literacy
Screenwriting

Foreign area

Afro-American
American Indian
Asian-American
Australian
British
Byzantine
Chinese
Classical studies
Demography
French
German
Human rights
International
Irish
Israeli
Italian
Italian-American
Japanese
Jewish
Norwegian
Polish
Scandinavian
Sikh
Spanish
United States
Welsh

Women's

Cosmetics
Fashion design
Health and beauty

Foreign language

Arabic
Chinese
Esperanto
French
German
Greek
Hebrew
Italian
Japanese
Latin
Mandarin
Portuguese
Spanish

History

American colonial
American
American Indian
Aviation / aerospace
British
Historical writing
Medical
Military science
Science
World

Law / legal

Business
Copyright
Criminal
Dispute resolution

Environmental
International
Law enforcement
Patent
Tax

Mathematics

Medical

Acupuncture / oriental medicine
Chiropractic
Dentistry
Health care administration
Homeopathy
Lab/clinical science
Optometry
Pharmacology
Pharmacy
Physical therapy
Podiatry
Public health
Speech pathology
Sports medicine

Medical research

Alcohol
Alzheimer's disease
Audiology
Biological psychiatry
Biomedical sciences
Birth defects
Cancer
Cystic fibrosis
Dental
Epidemiology
Epilepsy
Genetics

Gerontology
Immunology
Lupus
Mental health services
Mental retardation
Microscopy
Microanalysis
Neuroscience
Ophthalmology
Respiratory disease
Speech-language pathology
Strokes

Medicine

Anesthesiology
Family practice
Gynecology
Naturopathy
Neurology
Obstetrics
Orthopedics
Osteopathy
Pathology
Pediatrics
Psychiatry
Psychology
Radiology
Surgery
Urology
Veterinary

Music,

see Performing arts

Nursing

Anesthesiology
Behavioral science

Cancer nursing
Gynecology
Licensed practical nurse
Nurse assistant
Nurse practitioner
Obstetrics
Operating room
Pediatric
Physician's assistant
Registered nurse

Natural History

Anthropology
Archaeology
Back country
Museum studies
Historic preservation
Native American Indian
Paleontology

Nutrition

Cereal science/technology
Clinical dietitian
Culinary arts
Dietetics
Family and consumer science
Food management/science
Home economics
Human development

Performing arts

Accordion
Choral conducting
Choreography
Conducting
Dance
Drama

Drums
Guitar
Instrumental
Jazz
Music composition
Music management
Music performance
Opera
Orchestra
Organ
Piano
Religious music
Singing
String instruments
Trumpet

Philosophy/Theology

Physics

Political science

Arms control
Foreign policy
Government agencies
International relations
International peace and security
National security / national defense
Public administration / management
Public policy
Public service

Psychology

Behavioral science
Clinical psychology
Counseling
Developmental disabilities
Human sexuality

Mental health

Parapsychology

Rehabilitation counseling

Sports psychology

Sociology

Social service

Social studies

Social work

Sports sociology

Urban affairs

Vocational

Aviation

Auto mechanics

Baking science

Bartending

Computer technology

Cosmetology / barber

Electrician

Fire service

Flight attendants

Food service

Funeral service

Gardening

Gemology

Guide

Landscaping

Maintenance

Modeling

Musical instruments

Paralegal

Pilot

Secretarial

Truck driving

Vertical flight

Welding

JOBS, EMPLOYMENT AND CAREER INTERESTS

This is a step that may require you to take some time and do some outside Internet research before you actually search for scholarships.

Learn about the fields you are or might be interested in. Become aware of the range of alternatives people who work in those fields may enjoy. Do a search on the following search string:

<u>job titles list</u>

Go to the government and university Web sites that are identified in your search. Look over the lists and identify the titles or positions and identify the industries, positions, job titles, occupations, and vocations that interest you.

Study and identify specific areas that intrigue you.

Write these down. These become magic search words for your search strings.

<Positions>
<Titles>
<Occupations>
<Vocations>
<Industry Classification>

Identify the Potential Source
of Financial Aid You Are Interested In

Go after the organizations that interest you the most.

Go after the organizations that are likely to have financial assistance programs.

Go after organizations that are located in places where you would like to be.

Study the categories and magic search words below and identify the specific sources that may offer financial opportunities.

Write these down. Create a master list of *<Source Words>* that you will use for your particular search. These become magic search words for your search strings. Use your list and rotate through the *<Source Words>* you identify, searching for opportunities and information that will help you reach your goal.

GOVERNMENT AGENCIES

Government agencies have huge resources that continue getting better and better. You access them by entering the magic search word "government" plus the *<Learning Words>* and *<Internet Words>*. For example:

<u>US government online directories</u>
<u>US government online databases</u>
<u>US government agencies searchable index</u>

Government <Source>

A to Z   Agencies by name
Agencies by state   Directories

Databases
Locators
Personnel locators
Servers
Specialized databases
Specialized directories
Telephone directories
Government <Type>
International
National
Country
Federal
State
Regional
County
City
Local

Government <Branch>

Executive agencies
Legislative branch
Congress
House of Representatives
Congressional offices
Judicial offices
Governors

Government <Geography>

Country
State
Province
Region
County
City

Government <Subject>

You can also find government agencies by searching on the subject for which they are responsible:

Agriculture
Air
Airlines
Aviation
Business
Communications
Courts
Crime
Cultural
Demographics
Economic
Education
Employment
Energy
Environment

Health
Housing
Income
Labor
Laws
Legal
Libraries
Medicine
Natural resources
Regulations
Safety
Small business
Soil conservation
Statistics
Taxes

Telecommunication

Transportation

Water

Welfare

BUSINESS

<Companies>

<Corporations>

You can search for companies by using <*Learning Words*> and <*Internet Words*> along with the following words:

<Types>

Businesses

Companies

Corporations

Manufacturers

Services

Consulting

Example:

online directory business

online database medical companies

software companies a to z

Industry <Source>

A to Z

Associations by name

Association by state

Databases

Directories

Locators

Personnel locators

Servers

Specialized databases

Specialized directories

Telephone directories

<Industry>

Industry group

Industry by name

Industry classification system

Standard industrial code

SIC code

You can also search for companies by industry and by geography or location.

Company <Industry> <Location>

Known or general location
Country
Region
State
County
City

<Actual company name>

You can also search for an association by its actual name. When you find the individual company Web sites, you can look for people who can give you information about what you are looking for.

Executives
Offices
Departments
Divisions
Membership
Chapters

Company <News>

Company <Media Centers>

You can find out a lot of information about companies by visiting online media press centers. There you can view and often search for:

News releases
Press releases
Industry news
Competitor information
Competition information

News releases almost always contain contact names and phone numbers of senior executives, or public relations or external affairs personnel. Contact these people directly and ask them specific questions about whom you should contact to find out more about scholarship opportunities.

ASSOCIATIONS AND ORGANIZATIONS

Associations and professional trade organizations go by many names and can be searched in a number of ways.

<Synonyms and Related Words>

Associations
Organizations
Professional associations
Professional organizations
Trade organizations
Nonprofit organizations
Societies
Federations
Brotherhoods
Sisterhoods
Fraternities
Sororities

You can also search for associations using the *<Learning Words>* and *<Internet Words>*.

Example:

professional associations online database
nonprofit associations online directory

Once you get to an online database, directory or other type of invisible Web resource, you search the site with a specific subject or technical term.

Associations <Types>

Industry
Political
Advocacy
Labor
Social
Academic
Research

Technical

Trade

Cultural

Art

Once you are on an association Web site, you look for key information sources using the following words:

<Information Sources>

A to Z

Association by state

Chapters by location

Chapters by name

Databases

Directories

Locators

Personnel locators

Servers

Specialized databases

Specialized directories

Telephone directories

Associations <Industry>

Industry by name

Industry classification system

Industry group

Standard industrial code

SIC code

You can also search for industry by geography or location.

Association <Industry> <Geography>

Known or general location

Country

Region

State

County

City

<Actual Association by Name>

You can also search for association by their actual name. Once at an association web site you can find specific resources and information including:

Executives

Offices

Membership

Chapters

<Events>

Events represent special opportunities to identify and meet with people. Search for them and go to them.

Conferences
Conventions
Meetings
Seminars
Symposiums
Trade shows
Training
Workshops

EDUCATIONAL INSTITUTIONS

<u>Colleges></u>
<u>Universities></u>
<u>High Schools></u>

Colleges and universities have huge resources that continue to get better and better with time. You access them by entering the *<Education Word>* plus the *<Learning Words>* and *<Internet Words>*.

For example:

<u>schools online directories</u>
<u>universities online databases</u>
<u>colleges searchable index</u>

Once you get to specific university Web sites, you identify and look for scholarship information.

Current scholarship information is often posted at individual schools every year.

Specific application procedures, requirements, and even online applications are often available.

College or University <Source>

A to Z
School listings by name
School listings by state
Databases
Directories
Locators

Personnel locators
Servers
Specialized databases
Specialized directories
Telephone directories

Once you are on an educational institution Web site you can find a whole world of specific resources and information.

You must study and learn how to navigate the Web sites you find, as each one will be unique and different.

Identify Where You Want to Be and When

Search by location to identify specific opportunities that exist in specific places.

USE <LOCATION WORDS>

Identify your desired location and geography or places where you'd be willing to live.

Be open to opportunities everywhere and anywhere in your target fields of interest. Use the following magic search *<Location Words>* in your search strings:

Continent	Province
Abroad	Region
Country	County
State	City

USE <TIME WORDS>

Search by date to locate the most currently available information.

Be aware of the element of time—be aware of when things are due, and that start dates or end dates are key factors.

<Year>	<Day>
<Month>	<Deadline>

Research the Media to Identify Potential Sources of Information and Contacts

Media Web sites often have specialized directories, databases or search engines which allow you access to vast archived articles on key subjects of interest to you.

You can read and learn about your areas of interest. You can also search specifically for scholarships or job opportunities and identify specific organizations and contacts.

MEDIA

You access them by entering the *<Media Word>* plus the *<Learning Words>* and *<Internet Words>*.

A to Z	Personnel locators
Media by name	Servers
Media by location	Specialized databases
Media by state	Specialized directories
Databases	Telephone directories
Directories	Call letter
Locators	By format

Example:

<u>media online database</u>
<u>media online directory</u>

Go to media Web sites and then search for specific information.

Media <types>

Magazines	Radio shows
Trade publications	Radio stations
Newspapers	Radio syndicates
Daily newspapers	TV networks
Weekly newspapers	TV shows
Tabloid newspapers	TV stations
News networks	TV syndicates
News services	Cable shows
News syndicates	Cable systems
Radio networks	

Media <Industry Categories>

You can search on media industry categories in a number of ways. There are very extensive searchable and specialized directories and databases online.

You can identify the names, classifications or categories of industry that you are interested in and then search for the media that cover that topic.

Find them by searching using the *<Learning Words>* and the *<Internet Words>* with various specific industry names, categories or classifications, along with the media terms above.

Advertising, public relations and marketing	Farming
	Fashion
Architecture	Finance
Art	Food
Automotive	Forestry and logging
Aviation	Fraternal
Banking	Funeral
Beverage	Furniture
Book Trade, journalism, and publishing	Garden and landscape
	General interest
Building	Gifts, antiques and collectibles
Business	Government
Ceramics and glass	Health and fitness
Chemical	Healthcare
Cleaning and laundry	Hobby and craft
Computers	Home and garden
Concrete	Hotel, motel and hospitality
Conservation and ecology	Import / export
Cosmetics	Industrial
Country and western living	Instrument and control technology
Dairy Industry	Insurance
Dentistry	Jewelry
Department, chain and merchandise stores	Law and legal
	Lifestyle
Education	Marine
Electrical	Medical
Electronics	Men's magazines
Engineering	Metals
Entertainment	Military
Environmental	Mining

Music	Radio, TV and cable
Office	Railroads
Oil and gas	Real estate
Optical	Religion
Packaging	Restaurants
Paper	Science
Parenting	Sports
Pets and animals	Telecommunications
Pharmacy	Textile
Photography	Tobacco
Plastics	Transportation
Plumbing, heating and air	Travel
Power and energy	Women's
Printing	Woodworking
Purchasing	

Media <Specialty Editors>

Media specialty editors are responsible for generating the news or articles you read on a certain topic. You can search for them by name or title. They often go by one of the following titles, along with their particular area of specialty.

Editors
Reporters
Columnists
Correspondents
Specialty

You can select the specialty from this list:

Automotive	Communications
Banking	Computers / High Tech
Beauty / Grooming	Consumer Interest
Book Review	Economics
Building / Architecture	Education / Higher Education
Business	Electronics
Buyers Guide	Engineering
Careers	Entertainment / Arts

Environmental

European

Family / Parenting

Farm / Farming

Fashion

Features

Financial

Fishing

Fitness and exercise

Food

Golf

Guns / Shooting

Hardware

Health

Home

Hunting

Industry news

Interior design

International news

Internet

Investments

Lifestyle

Media business

Medical / Health

Multimedia

Networking

New product review

Nutrition

Outdoor

Personal computers

Personal finance

Photography

Popular music

Portable computing

Real Estate

Science

Seniors / Retirement

Small business

Software

Sports

Stock market

Telecommunications

Transportation

Travel

Wine

CREATE A SEARCH STRING

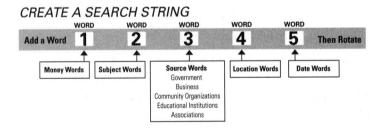

six

Getting Scholarships

Remember you are on a search with a special purpose. Once you identify a scholarship opportunity you need to apply for it.

To do this, you must have the essential information—who offers it, what it is, where it is, and how do you apply for it. This is the reality end of the business of scholarships.

This is the critical business information you are after.

Once you have this information you can apply.

Going from Ideas to Action

The Importance of Finding Critical Business Information (CBI)

You have to take everything you've learned and focus it on really going for the gold. By searching for specific financial opportunities we are about to put ideas into action.

Think of yourself as on a treasure hunt, searching for golden nuggets of information. You will capture these golden nuggets and turn them into real gold.

The Internet offers you access to expert information, news about companies, governments, organizations, and contact information. The primary goal of your whole Internet search effort focuses on uncovering "Critical Business Information" or CBI for short.

This is what you are ultimately after. Your search boils down to looking for:

(i)   Who to contact;
(ii)   What is the actual specific opportunity;
(iii) Where the opportunity is located; and
(iv)   How to apply and qualify for the opportunity.

Properly utilized, the critical intelligence forms the basis for action that can result in finding and applying for scholarships. You have to know **how** to look, and you have to know **what** to look for—and you also have to **know** it when you **see** it.

It really isn't hard. Most people who are hungry for information have "situational awareness" and they instinctively know critical business information when they see it or hear it:

If you are looking for a job:

"Ms. Smith just got funding for a new project."
"Joe just got promoted. His boss is desperate for a replacement."
"ABC Company is opening a new branch office in Houston."
"XYZ was just awarded a new contract in Seattle."

If you are looking for a scholarship:

The Black Women Engineers Society offers scholarships for minority women students in engineering, science, and technology.

If you are looking for an internship:

Microsoft Corporation offers summer internships for students at its Redmond, Washington campus.

If you are looking for a grant:

The National Endowment for the Arts accepts proposals from needy nonprofit organizations until March 15.

CBI is easy to spot when you see it or hear it. Just look for the who, what, where, when, and how.

However, CBI is not that always easy to come by. It is often disguised and buried in layers of Web pages and bureaucracy. Sometimes you have to investigate a little further or be inventive to create a missing piece of critical information.

What you really need to turn CBI into real opportunity is "how" to get what you want.

To illustrate this point, let me give you a simple lesson in economics.

KATIE'S BOUNCY BALL THEORY OF ECONOMICS

Katie is a typical bright energetic fifth grader, who has learned everything she needs to know about how to succeed in the world.

Katie loves bouncy balls. She has been collecting them for several years now. She has over 100 of them in every color and size imaginable. Each costs 25 cents.

She knows that she can buy them at certain restaurants. In order to get one, she invariably has to ask her parents for a quarter.

In response to her plea they invariably say, "You can have a quarter after dinner as long as you behave during the meal."

And of course, Katie is on her best behavior for the remainder of the meal. As soon as dinner is over, she asks for the quarter. Her parents say, "You behaved perfectly during the meal so here is a quarter."

She then dashes to the lobby, gets her bouncy ball, and returns gleeful and happy as she can be.

Katie is the perfect example of someone who understands how to use *critical business information* (CBI) to achieve financial success.

1. She knows what she wants [a bouncy ball].
2. She knows who offers it and where it is located [the restaurant].
3. She knows the source of funding [her parents].
4. She knows how she gets it [behave during dinner].
5. She completes the process perfectly and asks for a quarter [application process].
6. She receives her 25 cents [award].
7. She gets her bouncy ball [her goal and achievement].

This is Katie's Bouncy Ball Theory of Economics. This story illustrates a crucial point about how people of all ages achieve success.

What is amazing is that this same principle applies to finding all sorts of scholarships, or jobs, and other financial rewards you may seek.

The process only gets more complex because of the type of money, specific language and terminology of the field or subject, and the specific application process or requirements for each situation you find.

The Classical Use of Conventional CBI

Before the Internet, people searching for scholarships, job and career information, and business opportunities had to use paper sources of information.

They read newspapers, went to libraries, and visited government reading rooms for trade publications and other specialized materials all in pursuit of identifying those little tidbits of critical business information.

To get contact information people had to use telephone books, and huge, often out-dated, printed directories, by talking with employees, secretaries, human relations personnel, and librarians.

And it worked for them.

When people heard about an opportunity, they took action. They wrote a letter and sent in an application and a resume. They called or went to see the person offering the opportunity.

Traditionally it took a long, long time, with 30 to 50 "nos" before they came up with a "maybe" or a definite "yes"—a real offer.

The New Way to Get CBI

The processes and the tools and the skills people used before the Internet are still the same as you use now.

Sure, there are a few innovations-like Internet communications and e-mail, but these are basically just technological conveniences.

Realize this—they are simply advances in the technology of communication. Society has seen advances before: the mail to phone, phone to fax, fax to Internet, and most recently from Internet to wireless.

People continue to research to get information, but now the time it takes is shorter. They read written words in a greater variety of forms. They can exercise communications across a much wider network with other people, conducting informational interviews to find CBI.

Today, with the vast resources of the Internet and e-mail, this can be accomplished faster, easier and cheaper than ever before.

However, to apply and negotiate these opportunities, you still need to make phone calls, write letters, and send in applications, letters, and resumes, and conduct interviews. You still have to complete proposals and transmit them.

All this is still true. The actual search and decision-making processes that people go through is still the same.

It is up to you to take these actions.

CREATE A SEARCH STRING

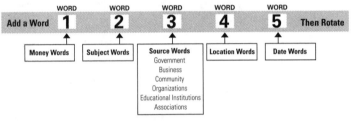

Search for CBI (Critical Business Information):
1. WHO to contact;
2. What is the specific opportunity;
3. Where is the opportunity located; and
4. How to apply and quality for the opportunity.

seven

The Magic Incantation

The Internet is a wonderful vast global storehouse of information. Almost all of what used to be available only on paper is now accessible through the Internet from the comfort of your home or office, plus it provides you with more variety than what was previously available.

With the advances in technology and the incredible growth of the Internet, critical business information is available on the Internet where people can access it 24-hours a day from anywhere in the world.

All you need is a portable computer and access to a phone. You can surf the Internet to your heart's content, and research all sorts of things that interest you.

Once you use the Internet to search for knowledge and identify real opportunities, it's time to take action.

The Four Steps: Search, Find, Match & Apply

This is the basic sequence of steps you will follow once you get in the swing of things.

You will repeat this sequence for as long as you use the Internet to find opportunities, whether they are scholarships or jobs, or other types of opportunities and information in other aspects of your life.

Search

Remember that you are searching with specific purpose and goal in mind: To find a specific scholarship opportunity. You are on a treasure hunt, and at all times you must remember what you are looking for and seek it out.

As you search, evaluate what you find. You must constantly look for a match between what you want and what you find.

Find

When you find places and organizations that interest you, evaluate them for scholarship opportunities.

Zoom in on the scholarship information and look for the real CBI. Look for the "what" first, and then look for the "who," "where," "when," and finally the "how."

Match

Stay focused and compare what you want with what you see. When you hit a "possible" there are several key questions you need to answer:

(i)   Does the opportunity meet your needs?

(ii) Do your qualifications satisfy their needs?

In other words, ask yourself, "Is it a match?"
Are the people, money, place, and time right for you?
Do you think you are right for them?
Only you can answer these questions.

Apply

When you find a match, you must first develop or acquire the specific and appropriate application materials. Then, prepare the application and send it in.

In some cases, you may find that you can submit an online application. More often, you will be able to find the online application instructions, guidelines, address, and application form online. These will have to be printed, and then prepared and submitted offline.

Implementing Your Action Plan

Staying on Target

You need to get to the key critical business information to take effective action. This may be hard to do.

As you evaluate for a match, remember that Web sites are built in a competitive market and advertising environment. Web sites often distract you in ways that will detract from you reaching your goal:

(i)   They seek to appeal to you emotionally.
(ii) They focus on selling you benefits and products and services you may not need, nor want, nor can afford.
(iii) They overwhelm you with off-target information.

You will encounter lots of facts, opinions, and information, which is nice, but useless for your specific purpose.

Remember to read with a purpose. Remember your goal and stay focused on finding and matching the critical business information to your needs.

Who, what, when, where, and how

If the information you see during your search adds to your information base, *SAVE IT, PRINT IT, BOOKMARK IT* so you can review it and act on it later.

If it doesn't, MOVE ON. Don't get diverted, stay focused. Evaluate what you read against your base of personal knowledge and experience.

When you find new information, savor it and be open to new ideas. Let new information CHANGE YOU. Think about what you can do with the new information, knowledge, or ideas. Free yourself to speculate a little. Use your imagination.

If you are worried that you will not be able to spot CBI, don't be. Great critical business information (CBI) will jump right off the computer screen at you. It will scream TAKE ME.

Your intuition plus your personal knowledge will help you identify the important information and match it to your goal. Pay attention when your intuition tells you that you may have a match.

Also, remember that the Internet is very personal. When you run across other people's stories, pay attention to their experiences, their successes, and their failures. Learn what you can from other people's strategies, tactics, techniques, experiences, and contacts. You may find that you can fit in where they cannot, or vice versa.

The most important thing to understand is that you are exploring a whole new universe of information. You can look for, find, and act on critical information. It is right there in front of you.

From the beginning to the end of your search, your efforts will bear the most fruit if you are careful, organized right from the beginning and deliberate. In the beginning you will lay out your plan of attack. This is important for being effective.

Your first few actions may or may not grab you with enthusiasm and satisfaction. Recognize that getting results quickly at the early stage of your research will make more of an impression on you than in later steps. Yet, finding the real CBI may not come in the early stage, but only after a relatively long and detailed search.

Therefore, be prepared for a long and tedious search. Don't expect too much too soon. Go slow to go fast.

Plan ahead

Making a plan of attack allows you to know—in advance—every major step in your research. Implement your strategy step-by-step.

However, recognize that you also get to do a wonderful thing. At every step you get to:

(i)   Follow your plan; or
(ii) Throw it out the window.

You can follow the plan you started, you can modify it as you go, or you can start all over and create a new plan. How you proceed depends on the CBI you find along the way.

Get to Closure

You will know when it is time to stop searching down a particular path or line of inquiry when you:

(i)   Find critical information,
(ii)   Identify and record an action, and then
(iii) Execute an action (*e.g.,* request information or apply for an opportunity).

You want to reach closure so you can end your search process and go onto something new with a feeling of completeness and accomplishment. You need to reach closure to feel good.

Review your search, the actions you initiated, and the submittals you completed. At the end of the search sessions, collect your thoughts and write them down.

If and when you need to return to this information, you will have these available readily. Your notes will help you pick up threads you discovered earlier

If you did not have time to explore, refer to your notes and pick up right where you left off and start searching again.

Maintain a Focused Sense of Humor

Staying sane while you are working online is a constant challenge. You will get tired of reading advertising and marketing hype. The Internet is a market-driven environment and hype is used to attract your attention. It also diverts you from your goal and wastes your valuable and limited time.

Handle these frustrations by maintaining a sense of humor while you read.

- Laugh at the unbelievable stuff your search engines find and isn't relevant.
- Laugh at the childish attempts of some people as they try to create Web sites and get traffic.
- Smile at other people's mistakes that you notice.
- Smile at your own mistakes when you make them and catch them.
- Be understanding of others and of yourself.
- Don't be content to be the same person you are today.
- Decide to act on your ideas, strategies and tactics.

You hold the power. Use it. When you find CBI, act on it.

Take Action

As you use the Internet and search for critical business information in your key target organizations, you will ultimately come down to one of two final actions. When you find what appears to be a match you can:

  (i)   Request the critical information, and
  (ii) Apply, apply, apply.

Let's look at this critical situation carefully.

Do you have all the information you need to apply? If not you must request this information. This could be a copy of the latest applications or the instructions so that you use the proper process and are successful.

When you write your letter requesting more information, tell them why it is important to you.

Request the Critical Information

If you are looking at what appears to be a match, and you have everything you need to apply or transmit the necessary information, you now need to take the final action.

Your Final Action = Apply, Apply, Apply

You can do this even when they are not advertising a vacancy or specific opportunity. You can do this because they may not even know they have a problem that you can solve until you contact them with your solution.

Make sure that you treat each final application action as a singular, important, and personal event. This is your life we are talking about. Take the action seriously.

When you send your cover letter, application, resume, or proposal, make sure these items are the best that they can possibly be. You are contacting real people who can help you immensely. Treat your contacts as special people. Give them extra special respect.

Don't just sit there—do something!

Call or visit people who do what you are thinking of doing. Take pictures of them in their workplace, talk with them, and visualize yourself being in a similar position. Do you really want to do this?

If yes, proceed ahead. If no, it's not a match, and you should do something else. Take an action.

Taking Action Will Bring You Closer to Success

If you are still interested:
- Identify and try to talk with prior scholarship winners. Learn what they did and how they got their awards.
- Identify and try to make an appointment to meet with the chairperson or member of the committee who evaluates the applications and decides on the winner.
- Prepare for the application process and plan an interview. Learn about who created the scholarship and why. Find out what the organization does and show interest in finding out more. Learn about the organizations history.

Taking action:
- Forces you to experience the consequences of your actions. It also gives you feedback that stimulates you to make a better decision and to improve the next time.

- Motivates you to take more actions and heads you in the direction that leads to your success. It makes it easier to remember information and easier to learn. And, most importantly, it forces you to apply the information wisely.
- Enhances the depth of your commitment to your goal.
- Allows you to fine tune your strategy as well as sharpen the tactics you use to achieve your goals. You learn what works, and you do it some more. By the same token, you learn what doesn't work, and you avoid repeating wasteful behaviors.

Taking action can change your attitude. Even as you begin to use the Internet you will find that you must give up preconceived notions in order to get the most out of the search and take full advantage of the capabilities of the Internet:

- Search engines are slow and useless.
- Everyone is not necessarily a crook.
- You thought that there's nothing out there for you.

Quality information is readily available, if you know how to look for it.

If you are really committed to succeeding, you will search, search, search and search some more.

However, try not to get hooked on just searching.

Make sure you apply, apply and apply some more.

Polish Your Application

Prepare the Best Application You Possibly Can

Once you find a possible match, all your energy should focus on the development and completion of your application materials and their timely delivery.

You must realize that how your application materials appear will determine whether or not you succeed.

If your application materials fail to provide what your target wants, all your efforts will have been wasted. Thus, you must make sure your application materials are:

   (i)   Complete.
  (ii)   Persuasive.
 (iii)   On time (before and not after the deadline).

The general appearance of your application tells people a lot about how you will perform as compared to others. To be better than the competition you must:

- Be professional
- Be distinctive
- Be prepared

You need to be competitive and competent. You do it by taking advantage of other people's indifference to the appearance of their application. Make yours stand out from the rest of the crowd of applicants by judicious use of color, paper, format, and possibly color pictures. Let your package convey your energy, intensity, enthusiasm, and your commitment to your goal.

If you aren't going to put real effort into your application, don't waste your time; don't even bother to apply.

Knowledge is power. The specific application of knowledge is applied power. See what you are doing as an application of applied power.

By searching, you are accumulating knowledge. Your application acts as a catalyst for change. Decisions involving hundreds, thousands, tens of thousands, hundreds of thousands of dollars are at stake and spin off your decision to apply.

Do not think that what you are doing is a waste of time. It is not. Here is what happens:

- You will write an e-mail asking for the application. After you receive it, you complete it and send it in.
- The organization receives it, reviews it, comparing applicants, deciding which person fits the best.

- The dollars flow from the organization to one of the people who applied.

You are only eligible if you are one of the people who applied on time. Pay close attention to application deadlines. Start your scholarship search efforts early, get your applications in order, and apply early.

Applying requires no special audience although you can, and should, seek help from reviewers. Speak to those who have gone through the same process successfully. Ask them questions about how they would improve their application or scholarship search if they were to do it again.

Before you submit your application materials, review them carefully. Get a professional critique. Look for and fix mistakes. Look for ways to improve your materials. Revise your materials again and again and again until they really begin to glow. Polish, polish, polish until they really shine and sparkle.

And then send it in. Apply.

Follow Up

Following Up Can Help You Close the Deal

The one final thing to do after coming this far is this:

Follow up.

Follow up.

Follow up.

Follow up.

And then follow up some more. This is something very few people do even though it can make the difference between success and failure. It is called the strategic follow up.

You follow up to make sure the organization received your application and that it contains everything that it is supposed to contain.

Call by phone, send a fax, write an e-mail telling everyone that you applied for the scholarship(s) and that you are checking on its status.

Get verification that everything is complete.

Once you get through, do one more last little thing.

Ask for the name or names of the actual decision-makers, and try to get to the decision maker and ask that person one crucial question:

"What else can I supply you in the way of additional information that will help me get selected?"

Phrase this question in a way that is comfortable for you.

Then, listen carefully. Record or take notes on what your prospect says.

Ask for his or her address.

Then, develop and submit this information immediately. Send it with an updated application via priority mail directly to the person you were talking to.

This is the strategic follow up.

Communicate with your key target sources. Ask good questions via e-mail before and after you apply.

Again, use the strategic follow up. Find out if they have everything they need to process your application. Get to the key decision-maker, introduce yourself, and make a personal pitch.

Even though you may be told everything is fine, you may learn something that will justify your transmitting additional information.

Find out if they'd like some more information.

Provide them with something extra, if you learn it can tip the decision your way.

It may make the crucial difference between success and failure.

Using E-Mail to the Max

Speaking of e-mail, there are special tactics you can use to successfully use e-mail communications on the Internet, which will aid your search immensely.

So use e-mail, and use it wisely.

If people like interacting with you online, they will treat you favorably. If you treat them well, they are far more likely to treat you well.

You've got to understand that the Internet and e-mail allow you to be personal and to customize and tailor your writing. However, it is up to you to explore and maximize the technology to communicate with your prospect. It is up to you to figure out just how well you can treat them using these tools.

WRITE BUSINESS QUALITY E-MAIL:

Become a student and dedicate yourself to becoming a skilled practitioner of "Business Quality E-Mail." It is perhaps the most critical element in the equation for successful Internet commerce.

With the Internet, the e-mail message sent to a prospect is often the spark that makes or breaks the relationship. E-mail is very personal. It lands on your computer screen 12 to 14 inches away from your eyes. It has tremendous psychological and personal impact.

We are acutely sensitized to unsolicited commercial e-mail (spam). We hate it! Yet, how many of us have devoted significant effort to honing and perfecting the e-mail responses we send to our friends, family, colleagues, Web visitors and business prospects?

Take care to write and respond personally and professionally to people that you encounter in your searches using the Business Quality E-Mail approach.

Don't send a standard boilerplate message via e-mail. Do not allow your e-mail to slip into a typically personal stream of consciousness-style so common in short snappy e-mail messages. If you do it, stop doing it now. Professional prospects respond better if you write with a more formal and respectful e-mail style.

Your e-mail should adopt a formal style and begin, "Dear Ms. Smith." Write slowly and carefully. Place the same care and effort into your e-mail response as if you were writing a formal letter with letterhead paper. Write to your prospect directly using the first person "I."

PROVIDE THEM WITH SOMETHING EXTRA

If they write back, especially in response to a formal request or proposal you have made, answer their specific questions, explore their line of inquiry, and always leave them with an enticing offer for more information.

Why an enticing offer? Because this gives your prospect yet another reason to continue her dialog with you and take another step.

This giving continues throughout the pre-application period, the actual application period, and beyond—where you seek to receive repeat scholarships or fellowships with the same organization and create an ever-expanding feeling of loyalty and total satisfaction in dealing with you.

Ask yourself—what else can I offer that will keep this person coming back for more?

What you can usually offer is to provide additional relevant, problem-solving, personalized information.

Your offer may be an extra bit of research or an expanded bit of writing or demonstration of your skills and abilities. You ask them "Would you like to see more of my work?"

The sincerity, helpfulness, personal and professionalism of your business quality e-mail will lead them on and they will continue to work with you. You will immediately distinguish yourself.

Over time you will incorporate the business quality e-mail approach into everything you do. You will find that on the Internet business quality e-mail communications really count.

But remember, not everyone has entered the new age of electronic commerce.

So if your e-mail doesn't seem to get their attention, call, fax, write a letter or visit in person. Figure out what it takes to be successful and do whatever it takes to achieve the necessary communications.

You can take a free online tutorial course in Business Quality E-Mail. Just open your browser and enter the Web site URL:

www.EmailtotheMax.com

Use the 3 1 Technique

Figuring out what your funding source wants is one of the most critical decisions you, as a scholarship opportunity seeker, can make.

In most cases, they will tell you very specifically what is required in the guidelines, information, or instructions. You, then, create and deliver precisely what you think they are asking for and then move assertively towards being selected.

Take advantage of what every good planner knows; how to take advantage of thinking three steps ahead, while proceeding one step at a time. Don't go for the moon all at once. Set a goal with each and every prospect; achieve it; and then build on that goal.

How do you do this? Use "The 3I Technique:"

Identify, Imitate, and Innovate

The 3I technique is by far the quickest and easiest technique you can use to develop the tools and skills you need to design and implement a successful scholarship search of your own. The 3I Technique consists of three simple steps:

1. Identify a success story.
2. Imitate the success story.
3. Innovate your own success story.

Let's take a look at these in more detail and learn how to apply this powerful technique.

Step 1: Identify a Success Story

When you search, keep an eye out for success stories. This is the story of someone who got what you are after. It could be a scholarship, a fellowship, or an internship, a job, or a contract. Whatever it was, it is exactly what you wish you could get.

When you find a success story, study it closely. Dissect the story looking to piece together the steps the person took to achieve that goal. Make sure that you make a list of the things the person did, and identify and describe the steps the person took.

You can search on the Internet for sample scholarship application and submission examples and samples. As you can probably figure out by now, the magic search words are:

scholarship application winning essays examples

scholarship application winning essays samples

past scholarship winners

Many organizations actually make publicly available the actual submissions for the winners. You can search for these, send in an e-mail request for them, or call the organization and find out where and how they can be viewed or acquired.

Create a search string using your particular identified funding source plus the words "prior winning applicants" or "winners."

Do your best to get them into your hands. Then, dissect them and use the 3 I Technique.

If possible, find a copy of the actual proposal, essay, or application materials the successful person submitted. Look closely at the exact instructions the person had to follow.

Investigate to find out as much as you can to see what this person really did. Search for other winning essays and applications from this and other sources. Learn what it takes to be successful. Study the winners. Learn from those who have been successful before you.

Save what you find from your research—build a file, make a scrapbook, create a binder—so you have this valuable information easily accessible.

Step 2: Imitate the Successful Process

Your goal is to understand the process, build a set of similar tools, and then develop and apply the skills, so you can repeat the success process. The way to accomplish this is straightforward:

- Study the application, proposal, and other written materials closely and see how the successful process was conducted.
- Study the types of written materials that were required.
- Make a checklist and get familiar with the style, length, focus, content, and word choice used in these written materials.

Get ready to create your own materials. Start writing by imitating the content, organization, and style of the written materials you see. Take them one at a time and parallel the writing you see, line by line, paragraph by paragraph, page by page. First imitate the cover letters, then the applications, the resumes, then the proposals or applications, then finally, the essays.

Step 3: Innovate the Final Materials

While imitation is a good first step, you now should seek to make improvements. Remember that you need to be aware of the correct process and the current guidelines, instructions, and required deliverables.

However, you also need to make your materials personal to you, so think about how you can do even better.

Thus, ask yourself how you can improve your materials and make them better than the examples you have before you. Think about how you can improve each of your tools. Now re-write your written materials.

In fact, re-write them again and again—revise, revise, and revise some more. Your written materials—your tools—have to sing to you before you send them in, if you are to make you the best effort you possibly can.

USE THE INTERNET TO YOUR ADVANTAGE:

Visualize the process and your position on your plan to keep on track.

While this book gives you a great structure for finding scholarships on the Internet, it is important for you to continually assess where you are, what stills needs doing, and where you need to go.

Look at what you are doing and identify to yourself what step in the process you are taking at every moment. Self-monitor your own progress—you cannot achieve satisfaction unless you know what you want.

1. Master the tactics, strategies, and use of "magic search words" to hone your skills and capabilities.
2. Use the search engines, directories, the specialized databases and libraries to search for opportunities.
3. Get the critical business information off Web sites.
4. Act to request the critical business information.
5. Once you have the CBI—apply, apply, apply.
6. Use the strategic follow up so you can always be ready to respond to an opportunity that didn't exist until you entered the picture.

The key here is to make sure you know what you want, learn what it takes to get there, create the tools, and develop the skills you'll need, and learn these well enough for you to act effectively as you go through the process. Your commitment to action will keep you focused, energized, enthused, and effective.

Conclusion

Hopefully, with the help of this *Magic Search Words* book, you will have learned to search the Internet for information that will improve your life.

As you go out and search for information, read with the purpose of using it right away.

Read for critical information. Plan on using it.

Be proactive with the information that you find.

Take action. Make sure that you use what you find.

Don't stop till you achieve success.

Avoiding Disaster

Identify and avoid scholarship search scams, fraud and abuse. If it seems to good to be true, it definitely is.

There are well known warning signs you can use to identify a likely scam:

- If they tell you you've won a scholarship, but you never applied, it's probably a scam.
- If they say it'll cost you money to match and find you a scholarship, it's probably a scam.
- If they say, they just need your credit card to hold the scholarship for you, it's probably a scam.
- If they say it's guaranteed and they'll do all the work for you, it's probably a scam.
- If they seek to charge you for just a search, it's probably a scam.

Don't get taken for a bum ride. Learn how to identify scams and fraudulent scholarship schemes. Do a search on the words:

SCHOLARSHIP SCAMS FRAUD

Study up on how to avoid getting caught in a trap. Learn what the government and watchdog agencies say about how to recognize a scam and qualify a search service.

Protect yourself.

How Good Is the Magic?
GIGO (Garbage In Garbage Out) or MIMO (Magic In, Magic Out)

You must evaluate the quality of the information on the web sites you find constantly. Before you assume that information is valid and factually correct, you should:

1. Determine its source origin. Discover the author, the publisher and the purpose of the web site.
2. Are they objective, unbiased, and independent? Or are they selling products or services? Do they have ulterior motives?
3. Determine the authors and publisher's credentials, expertise, and experience. Do the author's qualifications support their ability to provide factually correct information?
4. Identify the date of the writing to establish the historical context.

5. Verify it. Find at least one other reputable source that provides similar substantiating information.

Learn more about how to assess the quality and truthfulness of information on the Internet. Search on:

<u>evaluating the quality of information on the Internet checklist</u>
<u>assessing the quality of web sites information</u>
<u>identifying fraudulent, inaccurate and questionable web sites</u>
<u>quality of information on the Internet</u>
<u>criteria for evaluating web site information</u>

Parting Words

People often ask. "What is the best scholarship to apply for?" There is obviously no simple answer to this question.

Indeed, there are so many opportunities and options out there. No one could ever hope to answer the question because the answer depends on what you are willing to do.

What you search, find and apply for will depend on your wants and interests, and the time and energy you invest in the effort. Only you can determine what you want, need and are willing to do to get it.

Even if you land just one scholarship, you will have to start all over and keep on searching, finding and applying to get the next one.

If you stop searching, one thing is for certain, you'll get nothing more. If you continue searching, finding and applying, the odds are in your favor that you'll receive more.

Fortunately, the Internet and search engines have evolved so that information to help you find what you are looking for is right at your fingertips.

Search. Learn the key search techniques and become proficient at them.

Start searching. Do it and do it now. You have nothing to lose and a world of information and scholarships to gain.

Once you start, this is what will happen:

• You will discover and release a desire to find and utilize new resources within yourself. You will suddenly want to achieve new things in your life.

- You will become more knowledgeable, more competent, better trained, more creative, more skilled, and more adventurous.
- You will learn new things. You will come up with new ideas that will help you replace old self-defeating patterns of behavior and boredom. You will be able to use the new information, and improve yourself with new tool, skills and abilities.
- You will realize that knowledge is power. At every step, you will learn something new and something powerful.

What you can expect:

- You will act on that information and come closer to your goal.
- You will understand that the key to success in life is to take action on what you learn.

As you act, you trigger actions in others, and new information and new opportunities will come your way. Don't hesitate—act on them.

As you experience the thrill of creating these opportunities, you will develop a sense of wonder and respect for knowledge and a love and appreciation for learning.

Believe in creative reality. Make your dreams come true. Do it.

Search. Start your search knowing what you want. Visualize it as best you can.

Look at the steps in this book as a way to reach within yourself and use the amazing Internet resources that are available at your fingertips to create a new vision and a new reality for your life. This book can help you narrow your choices to a few outstanding opportunities worthy of your active consideration and effort.

Don't get hooked on relying on the scholarship search databases alone. They only dole out tidbits and no single database is all-inclusive.

You learn more by searching yourself and taking the actions needed to get more information directly from the source. You will be surprised that most of this information will be provided to you free of charge.

With a little dedication and some conscientious time and effort, you will discover the right scholarship opportunities. This is your life. Go for it.

Good luck and good searching!

PAUL J. KRUPIN
KENNEWICK, WASHINGTON

APPENDIX A

Your Scholarship Search Action Plan

Here is your scholarship road map. Using these bullets as a guide, create your own more detailed Scholarship Search Action Plan

- Learn about Search Engines
- Learn and practice searching your favorite subjects using
  - *<Learning Words>*
  - *<Internet Words>*
- Identify what you want in the way of scholarships and other forms of financial aid and using
  - *<Money Words>*
  - *<Job and Employment Words>*
- Identify and recognize who you are and what you want, e.g., your qualifications, characteristics and interests:
  - Personal and social characteristics
  - Education and personal interests
  - Career interests
  - Industry interests
- Search for the specific sources of financial aid:
  - Government agencies
  - Associations, organizations and institutions
  - Companies and corporations
  - Educational institutions
  - Community organizations

- Adjust your search to meet other personal needs or desires using:
  - *<Location Words>*
  - *<Time Words>*
- Search for *<Media>* and other information that will provide you with additional information and possible sources of knowledge and contacts.
- Search and find scholarships that match your needs and interests
- Focus on getting the Critical Business Information (CBI):
  - What
  - Who
  - When
  - Where
  - How
- Request Application Materials.
- Search for, request and study successful past scholarship winning applications, essays and other submissions.
- Use the 3 I Technique to create your applications.
- Apply on time.
- Follow up to make sure the application is received, is complete, and as good as it can possibly be.
- Repeat.

Summary of the Best Scholarship Magic Search Words

Learn about Search Engines

Search engines

Search engine watch

Search engine showdown

Search engine comparison chart

invisible web

invisible web tutorial

The Minus Dot Com Trick

-.com.

<Subject> <topic> ...-.com...

-.com .org

<Subject> <topic> ...-.com .org

Learning Words & Internet Words

<Money Words> <Learning Words> <Internet Words>

<Money Words> <Skill word> tutorial

<Money Words> online database

<Industry Words> online directory

<Source Words> searchable database

The Add a Word Technique

<Word Group 1> <Word Group 2> <Word Group 3> <Word Group 4> ...

Search String Word Groups

<Money Words>

<Job, Employment or Career Words>

<Personal Characteristic Words>

<Learning Words>

<Internet Words>

<Source Words>

<Skill Words>

<Document Words>

<Education Words>

<Industry Words>

<Location Words>

<Time Words>

The Search String Technique

<Word Group 1> <Word Group 2> <Word Group 3> <Word Group 4> ...

Search Word Rotation

<Money Word # 1> <Personal Interest Words> <Source Words> <Location Words> <Date Words>
<Money Word # 2> <Personal Interest Words> <Source Words> <Location Words> <Date Words>
<Money Word # 3> <Personal Interest Words> <Source Words> <Location Words> <Date Words>

Concept or Phrase Searching and Exact Quote Searching

Tips for applying for scholarships

Information in Different Languages/From Specific Countries

<Money Words> <Learning Words> <Internet Words> <Language Word> <Location Words>
<Money Words> <Learning Words> <Internet Words> <Country Code>

Searching to Improve General Knowledge

<Money Word> <Learning Words>
<Money Words> <Learning Words> <Internet Words>
<Money Words> <Learning Words> <Internet Words> <Source Words>

Searching to Improve Skills

<Money Words> <Skill Words> <Learning Words> <Internet Words>
<Money Words> <Document Words> <Learning Words> <Internet Words>

Searching for Specific Opportunities

<Money Words> <Industry Words> <Learning Words> <Internet Words>
<Money Words> <Personal Characteristic Words> <Learning Words> <Internet Words>
<Money Words> <Education Words> <Learning Words> <Internet Words>
<Money Words> <Major field Words> <Learning Words> <Internet Words>
<Money Words> <Minor field Words> <Learning Words> <Internet Words>
<Money Words> <Personal Interest Words> <Source Words> <Location Words> <Date Words>
<Money Words> <Sports Words> <Source Words> <Location Words> <Date Words>

Searching Specific Sources of Financial Aid

<Money Words> <Learning Words> <Internet Words> <Source Words>
<Source Words> online directory <Money Words>
<Source Words> online database <Money Words>
<Money Words> <Business Words> <Learning Words> <Internet Words>
<Money Words> <Government Words> <Learning Words> <Internet Words>
<Money Words> <Association Words> <Learning Words> <Internet Words>
<Money Words> <Organization Words> <Learning Words> <Internet Words>
<Money Words> <Community Words> <Learning Words> <Internet Words>
<Money Words> <Media Words> <Learning Words> <Internet Words>

Searching to Meet Specific Personal Needs or Desires

<Money Words> <Personal Interest Words> <Source Words> <Location Words> <Date Words>
<Money Words> <Industry Words> <Source Words> <Location Words> <Date Words>
<Money Words> <Education Words> <Source Words> <Location Words> <Date Words>

Index

3 I Technique, 95, 97, 104
About.com, 10
abuse, 99
action plan, 85, 103
action, 77–78, 88, 103
add a word, 16, 23, 25, 31, 105
advanced searches, 16
age words, 24
all about search engines, 7-13,
All the Web, 9
Alta Vista, 9, 17
ancestry, 42, 50–51
application, 33, 46–48, 71, 80,
    89–94, 96–97, 104
applications, 5, 33, 46, 71, 81,
    88–89, 92, 97, 104
apply, 41, 45, 77–78, 81, 84–85,
    87–93, 96–98, 104
Ask Jeeves, 11
associations and organization
    words, 25, 43, 69, 106
associations, 21–22, 30, 40, 43,
    47, 67, 69–70, 103
automatic plurals, 17
avoiding disaster, 99
boolean terms, 16
Britannica, 10
business quality e-mail, 93-94
business words, 43, 106
case sensitivity, 17
CBI, 77–81, 84, 86–88, 98, 104

CERN, 10
Chubba, 11
city, 29–31, 43, 66, 68, 70, 72, 111
colleges, 31, 47, 71
community organizations, 31,
    40, 42, 54, 103
companies & corporations, 30,
    40, 43, 47, 67, 103
companies by name, 30, 43
companies, 3, 12, 30, 34, 40, 43,
    47, 67–68, 78, 103, 112
concept searching, 45
conclusion, 99
corporations, 30, 40, 43, 47, 67,
    103
country or culture words, 24
creating search strings, 5, 23
critical business information,
    77–78, 80, 83, 85–86, 88,
    98, 104
culture words, 24
Cyber 411, 11
database, 8, 20–21, 31–32, 42,
    67, 69, 73, 102, 105–106,
    112
default settings, 17
desktop search utilities, 13
detailed phrase searching, 33
disability, 42, 53–54
Dogpile, 11
e-mail, 20, 81, 91–96, 112–113

education level, 29, 42, 53

education, 18, 24–25, 27, 29, 40, 42, 49–50, 53, 55–57, 59, 66, 71, 74–75, 103, 105–106

educational institutions, 31, 47, 71, 103

ethnic, 42, 50, 52

exact quote searching, 34, 106

Excite, 9, 17

family words, 24

federal government agencies, 30

field searching, 17

financial aid source words, 47

fraternal organizations, 31, 42, 54

fraud, 99–100

free stuff, 20

gender words, 24

geography and location words, 43

get to closure, 87

getting started, 4

going from ideas to action, 77

Google, 5, 8–9, 17–18, 23, 34–35, 38

government agencies, 3, 10, 20, 30, 34, 43, 47, 63, 65–66, 103, 112

government words, 43, 106

government, 3, 10, 18, 20, 30, 34, 40, 43, 47–48, 63–66, 74, 80, 100, 103, 106, 111–112

handicap, 42, 53

hobbies, 42, 50, 55

Hotbot, 8–9

how to use this book, 4

humor, 87–88

improve your general knowledge, 44, 47–48

index, 7–9, 20, 42, 65, 71, 107, 109

industry words, 25, 43, 105–106

Inference Fund, 11

institutions, 10, 30–31, 47–48, 71, 103

Internet words, 21, 25, 31, 38, 40, 42, 44–45, 65, 67, 69, 71, 73–74, 103, 105–106

Iwon, 9

job, career and employment words, 47, 50

Katie's Bouncy Ball Theory of Economics, 79–80

kids search engines, 13

language, 35, 42, 51, 59–61, 80, 106

learning words, 19–20, 25, 31, 38, 40–41, 44–45, 65, 67, 69, 71, 73–74, 103, 105–106

location words, 25, 43, 48, 72, 104–106

Looksmart, 10

Lycos, 9, 17

Magellan, 9–10

MagicSearchWords.com, 5, 113

major fields, 42, 55–56

major search engines, 12, 17

Mamma, 11

match, 16, 84–86, 88–90, 100, 104

media words, 25, 43, 106
Meriam-Webster, 19
Meryl K. Evans, ix
meta–search engines, 11
Metacrawler, 11
metacrawlers, 13
Metafind, 11
Microsoft Internet Explorer, 4
minor fields, 42, 50, 55–56
minorities, 33, 50
minus signs, 17
money words, 24, 28, 40, 42,
    44–48, 50, 103, 105–106
Mozilla, 4
multi–search engines, 11
Netscape Navigator, 4
Netscape, 4, 10
news search engines, 13
nonprofit organizations, 30, 47,
    69, 79
One2seek, 11
Open Directory, 10
Opera, 4, 63
operators, 16
organizations, 3, 18–19, 30–32,
    34, 40, 42–43, 47–48, 54,
    65, 69, 73, 78–79, 84,
    88–89, 96, 103
overview, 1, 39
paid listings search engines, 12
parting words, 100
personal characteristic words,
    24, 42, 105–106
philanthropic foundations, 30
phrase searching, 17–18, 32–33,
    106

plan ahead, 86
plus signs, 17
professional and trade
    associations, 30
professional associations, 47, 69,
    112
proximity searching, 17
purpose, 2
religion, 42, 50, 52, 75
resumes, 20, 46, 81, 97
reward search engines, 12
robot, 8
scams, 33, 99–100
schools, 20, 31, 34, 40, 71
search engine comparison chart,
    12, 105
search engine resources, 12
search engine showdown, 12,
    105
search engine watch, 12, 105
search string word groups,
    24–25, 30, 33, 40–41,
    44–45, 105
search strings, 2–3, 5, 10, 12, 16,
    20–21, 23, 29, 35, 38, 41,
    45, 49, 51, 55–56, 64–65, 72
search tool, 8
search word rotation, 2, 27–28,
    38, 44–47, 106
sense of humor, 87–88
simple phrase searching, 32
simple searches, 15
skills, 41, 106
software, 13
source words, 25, 31, 38, 47–48,
    65, 105–106

spaces, 17
special tactics for creating search
    strings, 23
specialized search databases, 11,
    13
specialty search engines, 13
specific goals for searching, 41
spider, 8, 13
sports, 30, 42, 45, 50, 55, 58, 62,
    64, 75–76, 106
stop words, 17, 34
synonyms, 24, 28, 38, 44, 47, 69
taking action, 89–90
the 3 I Technique, 95, 97, 104
the 3W Virtual Library, 10
the four steps, 84
the invisible web, 11
the Library of Congress, 10
the minus dot com trick, 18–19,
    105

the search string technique, 3,
    15, 105
thesaurus, 24, 42
time words, 25, 43, 72, 104–105
trade associations, 30
trade groups, 31
true search engines, 7–9
tutorial, 12, 19–21, 46, 95, 105,
    112
universities, 3, 10, 20, 31, 34, 45,
    47–48, 71
using e-mail, 93
virtual libraries, 10–11
web directories, 9
web directory, 9
Webcrawler, 9
wild card truncations, 17
Yahoo, 10
year, 25, 29–30, 42~43, 50, 53,
    71~72, 112

Who is Paul J. Krupin?

Paul J. Krupin is a scientist and "once-upon-a-time" attorney. He has over 28 years of diverse professional government and industry experience in a variety of technology and project management disciplines at complex industrial, nuclear, waste management facilities. He has been employed with the State of Oregon, U.S. Department of Interior, U.S. Department of Agriculture, U.S. Department of Energy, several law firms, and private industry. He was an emergency medical technician (EMT) and a County Civil Defense Director in Idaho. Paul has spent a lifetime dedicated to helping the government, business, industry, small business and individuals come up with creative systems and innovative solutions to complex policy, legal, regulatory, and technological problems and challenges. He has worked on solving or contributing to the solutions of some of the world's worst pollution problems. His adventurous career in government infected him with a love of public service.

Born in New York City, he was raised in Franklin Square on Long Island. He received a Bachelors Degree from the University of Colorado in Boulder, Colorado, a Masters Degree from Oregon State University in Corvallis, Oregon, and a Juris Doctor with a special certificate in Dispute Resolution from Willamette University in Salem, Oregon.

In 1992, after vowing to never step into a courtroom again, Paul devoted his newly found spare time to becoming an author, publisher, Internet innovator, and professional problem solver. He has come up with numerous highly innovative Internet systems and solutions. He loves to identify and develop what he calls "technological force multipliers", which in his own words are, "success pathways en masse, made easy to use with technology."

He is a prolific writer whose pre-Internet creations included the Toll Free Environmental Directory which taught people how to search for environmental jobs and information using toll-free numbers. He also wrote several fishing, hunting and archery books. He created several very popular highly specialized databases for government contractors including the National 8 A Minority and Economically Disadvantaged Company Directory & Databases series, Fed-Pro: The Federal Procurement Database, and DOD-Pro: The Department of Defense Procurement Database.

He discovered the Internet in 1994 and created a widely known media e-mail database called The US All Media E-Mail Directory. In 1996, he co-created, with Don Short of One World Telecommunications, IMEDIAFAX The Internet to Media Fax Service (www.Imediafax.com), an online service that allowed people to create their own custom targeted media lists and transmit them via fax and e-mail. Through IMEDIAFAX he has sent out millions of news releases each year. His clients include world-class companies, government agencies, professional associations and best selling authors on everything from *Chicken Soup for the Soul* to publicizing Internet and industry events to hard news journalists to syndicated columnists to electronic newsletters. Krupin's work is highly regarded in the publishing industry for his innovative Internet expertise and publicity achievements. He has touched the hearts and minds of millions of people.

The success stories and tactics of this remarkably successful Internet publicity service is chronicled in the highly rated book *Trash Proof News Releases*. He has developed sure-fire, proven strategies for getting publicity. His book covers the entire gamut of the how, why, when and where of news release construction, delivery and follow-up in today's fast evolving media environment. His book tantalizes you with real life PR success stories and proven tactics. His methods and services have helped hundreds of authors reach out to millions of people again and again.

Another of his Internet inventions is called www.EMailtothe-Max.com, a free online tutorial which teaches business people how to avoid email liability and improve their Internet and email skills, productivity and capability in what he calls "Business Quality Email." For creating this remarkable free service, he was featured on CNN Financial.

The *Magic Search Words* series evolved out of a problem he identified in 1999. No one knew how to use search engines. He set to work and created a new concept that helps people learn how to identify and select the best words to enter in search engines to get the best information quicker and easier than ever before. The original book, called *Finding the Gold Online,* covered everything from kids' homework to teen competitions, scholarships, jobs, personal finance, business finance, and venture capital, all the way to retirement money. Mainstream east coast publishers rejected this book as all too encompassing and suggested that single topic books be created. Hence, the *Magic Search Words* Series with individual books dedicated to single topics was developed.

Paul derives his greatest personal satisfaction by touching and improving the lives of people. His goal is to help millions of people by giving them quicker and easier access to the best information on the Internet. With the creation of the Magic Search Word series, Paul is embarking on a global campaign to teach people how to get better information off the Internet than ever before. He feels most people believe that helping themselves using the Internet is more than just for fun, a job, or a career, it is a now a core value. Like the library was for our parents, the Internet has now become and will remain an intrinsic part of our lives and a significant factor that will affect the future of all humanity. He is a man with a vision, a heart, and a soaring spirit that is an inspiration to all who seek to improve themselves and the world around them.

To contact Paul for further information or to schedule him for a speech, training seminar, or workshop, please contact:

Direct Contact

P. O. Box 6726

Kennewick WA 99336

Tel: 509-545-2707 or 1-800-457-8746 Fax: 509-582-9865

To send e-mail write to info@MagicSearchWords.com or visit www.MagicSearchWords.com

Get in Direct Contact—Quick Order Form

Fax Orders: 509-582-9865. Send this form.
Telephone Orders: Call 1-800-457-8746 toll free.
Or 509-545-2707. Have your credit card ready.
email Orders: orders@MagicSearchWords.com
E-Books: Visit MagicSearchWords.com
WWW.MagicSearchWords.com
Internet: Visit MagicSearchWords.com
WWW.MagicSearchWords.com
Postal Orders: Direct Contact Publishing, Paul Krupin, PO Box 6726,
Kennewick WA 99336 USA, Tel: 509-545-2707

Please send the following books or products. I understand that I may return any of them for a full refund - for any reason, no questions asked.

_____ Quantity _____

_____ Quantity _____

_____ Quantity _____

_____ Quantity _____

Please send more FREE information on:

- ❑ Quantity/Premium Orders
- ❑ Other Books
- ❑ Speaking/Seminars/Workshops
- ❑ Mailing Lists
- ❑ Consulting
- ❑ Fund Raising

- ❑ Custom Programmed Magic Search Pages
- ❑ E-Mail & Web Based Training Courses
- ❑ News Releases & Media Kits
- ❑ The Magic Search Word Column
- ❑ Getting Publicity with IMEDIAFAX—The Internet To Media Fax Service

Name:_____

Address: _____

City: _____ State: _____ Zip: _____

E-Mail Address: _____

Sales Tax: Please add 8.5 % for products shipped to Washington State addresses.

Shipping by US Priority Mail: U.S. $5.00 for first book and $2.00 for each additional book or product. International: $10.00 for first book and $5.00 for each additional book or product.

Payment: ❑ Cheque ❑ Credit Card — ❑ Visa ❑ MasterCard ❑ AMEX

Card Number _____

Name on Card:_____

Exp. Date: _____

Address of Cardholder: _____